Almost
EVERYTHING

ALSO BY ANNE LAMOTT

NONFICTION

Operating Instructions: A Journal of My Son's First Year

Bird by Bird: Some Instructions on Writing and Life

Traveling Mercies: Some Thoughts on Faith

Plan B: Further Thoughts on Faith

Grace (Eventually): Thoughts on Faith

Some Assembly Required: A Journal of My Son's First Son
(with Sam Lamott)

Help, Thanks, Wow: The Three Essential Prayers

Stitches: A Handbook on Meaning, Hope and Repair

Small Victories: Spotting Improbable Moments of Grace

Hallelujah Anyway: Rediscovering Mercy

FICTION

Hard Laughter

Rosie

Joe Jones

All New People

Crooked Little Heart

Blue Shoe

Imperfect Birds

Almost EVERYTHING

Notes on Hope

Anne Lamott

RIVERHEAD BOOKS

NEW YORK

2018

RIVERHEAD BOOKS
An imprint of Penguin Random House LLC
375 Hudson Street
New York, New York 10014

The author gratefully acknowledges permission to quote Lucille Clifton,
"blessing the boats," from *The Collected Poems of Lucille Clifton.*
Copyright © 1991 by Lucille Clifton. Reprinted with the permission
of The Permissions Company, Inc., on behalf of
BOA Editions Ltd., www.boaeditions.org.

Library of Congress Cataloging-in-Publication Data

Names: Lamott, Anne, author.
Title: Almost everything : notes on hope / Anne Lamott.
Description: New York : Riverhead Books, 2018.
Identifiers: LCCN 2018013899 | ISBN 9780525537441 (hardcover) |
ISBN 9780525537571 (ebook)
Subjects: LCSH: Spirituality. | Hope—Religious aspects. |
Life—Religious aspects.
Classification: LCC BL624 .L35195 2018 | DDC 170/.44—dc23
LC record available at https://lccn.loc.gov/2018013899
p.   cm.

Printed in the United States of America
1   3   5   7   9   10   8   6   4   2

BOOK DESIGN BY AMANDA DEWEY

For Neal Allen

CONTENTS

(at St. Mary's)

may the tide
that is entering even now
the lip of our understanding
carry you out
beyond the face of fear
may you kiss
the wind then turn from it
certain that it will
love your back   may you
open your eyes to water
water waving forever
and may you in your innocence
sail through this to that

— Lucille Clifton, "blessing the boats"

Almost
EVERYTHING

PRELUDE

I am stockpiling antibiotics for the apocalypse, even as I await the blossoming of paperwhites on the windowsill in the kitchen. The news of late has captured the fever dream of modern life: everything exploding, burning, being shot, or crashing to the ground all around us, while growing older has provided me with a measure of perspective and equilibrium, and a lovely, long-term romance. Towns and cities, ice fields, democracy, people—all disappear, while we rejoice and thrive in the spring and the sweetness of old friendships. Families are tricky. There is so much going on that flattens us, that is huge, scary, or simply appalling. We're doomed, stunned, exhausted, and overcaffeinated.

And yet, outside my window, yellow roses bloom, and little kids horse around, making a joyous racket.

In general, it doesn't feel like the light is making a lot of progress. It feels like death by annoyance. At the same time, the truth is that we are beloved, even in our current condition, by someone; we have loved and been loved. We have also known the abyss of love lost to death or rejection, and that it somehow leads to new life. We have been redeemed and saved by love, even as a few times we have been nearly destroyed, and worse, seen our children nearly destroyed. We are who we love, we are one, and we are autonomous.

Love has bridged the high-rises of despair we were about to fall between. Love has been a penlight in the blackest, bleakest nights. Love has been a wild animal, a poultice, a dinghy, a coat. Love is why we have hope.

So why have some of us felt like jumping off tall buildings ever since we can remember, even those of us who do not struggle with clinical depression? Why have we repeatedly imagined turning the wheels of our cars into oncoming trucks?

We just do.

To me, this is very natural. It is hard here.

There is the absolute hopelessness we face that everyone we love will die, even our newborn granddaughter, even as we trust and know that love will give rise to growth, miracles, and resurrection. Love and goodness and the world's beauty and humanity are the reasons we have hope. Yet no matter how much we recycle, believe in our Priuses, and abide by our local laws, we see that our beauty is being destroyed, crushed by greed and cruel stupidity. And we also see love and tender hearts carry the day. Fear, against all odds, leads to community, to bravery and right action, and these give us hope.

I wake up not knowing if our leader has bombed North Korea. And still, this past year has been just about the happiest of my life.

So yeah: it can all be a bit confusing.

On the one hand, there is the hopelessness of people living in grinding poverty in sub-Saharan

Africa, and uptown Oakland. On the other, we pour our money and time into organizations that feed and mentor people, teach in Uganda and Appalachia, show up in refugee camps with water and art supplies. People like us all over the world teach girls auto repair and electrical installation, teach boys to care for babies. Witnessing this fills me to bursting with hope. I have never witnessed both more global and national brutality and such goodness in the world's response to her own.

And then there are our families of origin. Some of us grew up in the alternative universe of unhappy marriages, where we accepted as normal desperate parental need, and bizarre sights just short of a head on a stick. I'm sure your family was just fine, and the template of love you grew up with was kindness and mutual respect, delight in each other, patience with a spouse or a child's foibles. But other families—just a few, here and there, hardly worth mentioning—were stressed, neglectful, fundamentalist, racist, alcoholic, schizophrenic, repressed. Brothers and sisters didn't always survive. We became jumpy perfectionists.

Almost Everything

T. S. Eliot wrote, "Teach us to care and not to care / Teach us to sit still." We long for this, and yet we check our smartphones every ten minutes for news, texts, distraction.

I wish that before my wise father died, at fifty-six, he had written down everything he had learned here, all the truths he was pretty sure of. He wrote many books of knowledge but not so much truth. Along with several fatal flaws, mostly involving women, he had several excellent rules: Don't be an asshole, and try to remember people's names, especially those people with no power or cachet, and seek beauty through binoculars, books, records. But truth? What did he know that might have helped his children steer their boats a little straighter? Not so much. He eschewed the spiritual life, except as his human spirit was sustained by nature, jazz, books, wine. A role model isn't a mentor. Life gave me mentors, though—poetry, pastors, the women's movement, naturalists, and friends—who helped me come to know several truths of which I am almost sure.

Just before my sixty-first birthday, I decided to make a list for my grandson and niece, who are both exuberant and worried, as I was at their age and still am some days—in fact, right now.

My Dearest, I began: I have had a spiritual mentor named Bonnie for three decades now, who loves me and trusts God and Goodness so crazily that I sometimes think of her as Horrible Bonnie, because I cannot get her to judge me or abandon hope. For thirty years, she has answered all of my distressed or deeply annoyed phone calls by saying, "Hello, Dearest. I'm so glad it's you!" I've come to believe that this is how God feels when I pray, even at my least attractive.

So, Dearest, I began: Here is everything I know about almost everything, that I think applies to almost everyone, that might help you someday.

After writing those words, I stalled. *What do I know?*

I do know two specific truths about me. One is that over the course of my life I have idly thought of jumping from rooftops and out of cars.

Late last night, for instance, my wonderful boyfriend was driving me home from the airport, where he had picked me up after I had flown in from officiating at the happiest wedding I'd been to in years, for a woman of thirty-five I adore. Neal was happy to pick me up because he had missed me so, although I had actually flown out only that morning. We were speeding across the Golden Gate Bridge to our funkily delicious home, where our animals awaited, and I was studying the diamond lights of San Francisco's bay and skyline, when the thought arose within me to open the door of his car and jump.

I was glad to be alive, in San Francisco, with Neal, and the car was going fifty miles an hour.

I rolled my eyes: Oh, you again. It was my mental roommate.

Over the decades, when it hasn't been this thought, it's been the one where I idly whip the steering wheel of the car and plow into a tree or big rig. I suppose this makes me sound at least a little angry, and we will save this for another day.

Of several mental health diagnoses I have received over the course of my life, one I don't actually have is depression. I have crippling anxiety, OCD, even clinical paranoia—yes, like dear old Richard Nixon—but not depression or suicidal ideation.

Well, unless you consider a lifelong obsession with jumping from high places to be "suicidal," which I don't particularly.

I have just always found it extremely hard to
be here, on this side of eternity, because of, well,
other people; and death.

The first time I felt the tremendous pushmi-
pullyu of anxiety about jumping, I was six years
old, and I was with my mother and brothers in
San Francisco. My mom was holding baby Stevie
inside the dentist's office, standing beside my big
brother as he got a cavity filled, while I was in the
waiting room trying to focus on *Highlights for
Children* in order to avoid studying the corner
window. (This is back when windows opened.)
We were fourteen floors up, and a magnetic force
in me was trying to pull me across the carpet to
the window. And I wanted to go. I had to dig in,
like someone in a game of tug-of-war or a dog
resisting the bathtub. That day I won, barely.

Forty years later, my psychiatrist Rick and I
made a deal. Whenever I was in any kind of ele-
vation outdoors or in a tall building with windows that opened, I was to tell whoever was with

me that I was idly thinking of jumping. This would break the trance and the tension, the power of keeping it a secret, moving toward it or backing away, like a girl trying to gauge the exact right moment to step under the arch of a jump rope swung by friends.

As you might expect, this admission tended to throw off my companions, who saw it as a buzzkill.

I've felt like jumping—or worried that I might jump—off bridges, the Empire State Building, a balcony overlooking a Mardi Gras parade. Every time, I have dutifully told my companions, who usually want to have little talks about the preciousness and challenges of life, permanent solutions to temporary problems, blah blah.

Only three words spoken at these times have ever helped.

A Coptic minister in Cairo once invited me to Egypt to give a lecture and a sermon, first at the American University, and then at his church in Maadi, outside the city. At dusk on my second day, he drove me up Mokattam Mountain, which is really a hill about five hundred feet high, at the base of which live as many as thirty thousand garbage workers, who gather Cairo's garbage and sort it there, ordering it into neat stacks and bundles on rooftops—plastic, cardboard, paper, metal. Farther up the hill, a church was created inside a cave, with seating for several hundred, and artists carved massive biblical figures into the rock face of the hillside. From the church there is an exhilarating view of the sprawling city, where ancient Egypt meets Islam and Coptic Christianity, with minarets, mosques, crosses, and in the distance the pointed peaks of the pyramids. The North African light is shadow and brightness, illuminating and obscuring, mesmerizing and mind-bending.

When we got to the church, the minister and I got out of his car, and before going inside, we walked to within a few yards of the cliff's edge, above Garbage City.

It was thrilling: the wild and pungent scene way below, donkeys and men pulling carts of garbage, women and children arranging it in piles and putting it into dumpsters, music and crosses and the hope of food that great industri-

ousness brings. Of course I thought about jumping. How could I not?

I cleared my throat and said shyly to the
minister: "I have to tell you something sort of
embarrassing. I promised my psychiatrist I would
tell whomever I was with when I was in any high
place that since childhood, whenever I'm very,
very high up, I think about jumping."

He didn't miss a beat. Waving away my con-
cern, he said, "Oh, who doesn't?"

And I could see again—the lights of the city,
children sorting garbage below, the slum, liveli-
hoods, men, donkey carts.

The second thing I know about myself is that
I have seen miracles, actual miracles, where people who have been given no chance of living
have lived, and in some cases are living still.

I know two families quite well who have lost
two out of three children. One of these families
had hosted the exuberant wedding I mentioned;
the other family I'm actually related to.

My cousins, with whom I grew up, had an
aunt Janet, with whom we were all in love. She
was the sister of my very beloved uncle Millard,

the tall, skinny man my mother's twin sister married, so she wasn't "our" aunt, but in the truer sense, Janet was ours because she was always around and she loved my family so. We saw her at every holiday. She was hilarious, very thin, beautiful in a tomboy way, joyously married to a shy and loyal engineer, and was the mother of three. She always joined in with the drinking and repartee.

Then one of her sons died suddenly when he was twelve, of an aneurysm. It was the end of the world. The whole family was crushed. Janet must have been as flattened as a tender green shoot. How can one possibly come through something so horrible? Parents are blown over by something this catastrophic—how can they not be?—and their roots barely stay in the shifting soil. But life holds on. Little by little, nature pulls us back, back to growing. This is life. We are life.

And we're rarely all alone. People come and go in our lives, surround us with their best selves, take us to the beach, to a bookstore, out for ice cream. So little bits of life and grace, time, habits, duties, a phone call, more time, all filter in to the seed under the concrete. And that seed pushes up through, no matter what, because this is how life is constructed—to live.

Many years after her son died, Janet was diagnosed with inflammatory breast cancer, and given a year at most to live.

She did all the chemo and radiation she could take, and then all the alternative modalities, too: supplements, deep meditation and affirmations. She went to New Age healing clinics, where the basic teaching was that love is the only truth, and that truth heals. She and I almost alone in our big family shared a belief that we were spiritual beings having human experiences, not vice versa, and that spirit, love, and truth were actual reality, superseding the vagaries of our physical realities. Everyone else teased us, calling us the woo-woo twins.

Then she started to get better. Months passed and her strength and color returned, and the cancer receded, visibly. She and her quiet husband, Ray, started to go line dancing again, every week.

She missed a holiday after her diagnosis, and

then the next Christmas she showed up at my uncle Millard's house. We were all gobbling down dip, gravlax, and bourbon, enjoying the banter, insults, one-upmanship, and erudite highbrow humor that defined our family. She grew quiet.

Then she asked for our collective attention. She said that things had changed for her now that she was fighting for her life. Her healing was dependent on loving environments and feedback, on continually giving and receiving love and positivity, and avoiding stress as much as possible. Therefore, she needed us to make a decision as a family whether we wanted to keep up our hilarious but hostile ribbing, and self-doubt disguised as humor, which she had always loved and enjoyed and participated in, or whether we wanted her to join us for our family gatherings, in which case we needed to change to a better station, with more love, listening, and gentler humor.

We picked her.

As a result, our holiday meals were definitely less wild and erudite and amusing, but we had

Janet's life and company. It was still fun, although less exhilarating and edgy. We changed.

We can change. People say we can't, but we do when the stakes or the pain is high enough. And when we do, life can change. It offers more of itself when we agree to give up our busyness.

It was great to be with Janet and my wild-horse family, gentled. Then she lost her other son, at the age of twenty-four, in a freak accident in Sweden. He was Cliff Burton, bass guitarist for Metallica. He was Janet and Ray's older son, Millard's nephew.

The bottom dropped out again. We all thought we knew the truth: that no one can survive the loss of two children without bitterness and rage, especially not someone fighting for her life with peace and happy thoughts.

Yet Janet lived five more years. She was coached, and she coached others, to do radical, active self-love, and to live in the light, not the dark of the sad past. She very much felt the love and support of her two sons nearby, not as ghosts or angels, but as living presences inside her. As a conscious act she did not dwell in their deaths. She looked forward to being with them again. She courted joy and gratitude, and meditated, which seemed to work, or at least help, and then at the end, took Laetrile, which didn't. But she lived, fully, beautifully, with sorrow and joy. She went line dancing with Ray a month before she died.

So the light did win this one. I believe that this family got its miracle, so much love and joy marbled into the cold and impossible.

Light not only warms, of course, but illuminates both things we want to see and don't want to see. Like the North African light, our inner incandescence reveals the hallucinatory and the ordinary, the magic and the grim. Light is energy you can't touch or corral, which is also the nature of spirit. They are both slippery, and slide around in every direction, and they are not always warm and fuzzy, which is so awful. I have felt ectoplasmic flickers of my father and best friends, life forces that have been snuffed out in the human realm but exist, like candles in another room. I once laughed in Safeway at something my friend Pammy said to me right that minute in the spaghetti sauce aisle, a year after she'd died. Light is drawn to light, like heliotropic flowers, poppies, marigolds—paperwhites. And us. Light, candles, full moons magnify spirit that is in the wings. That is a neat trick, to magnify the invisible, and it raises the question: Is there another room, stage left, one we cannot see? Doesn't something happening in the wings argue a wider net of reality? If there are wings off to the side or behind us, where stuff is unfolding, then reality is more than we can see and measure. It means there are concentric circles rippling out beyond the life we see being acted out on the stage.

I believe there is another room, and I have experienced this reality beyond our agreed-upon sense of actuality. But that's just me, with perhaps an overeager spiritual imagination and a history of drugs. I don't actually know that a deeper reality exists, but I believe that it does, and at least I know to pay attention to the light.

I'm pretty sure of several other things, beliefs that may be true. So, Dearest: Here is almost everything I know.

ONE

Puzzles

All truth is paradox. Everything true in the world has innate contradictions. "I know one thing, that I know nothing," Socrates said.

This is distressing to those of us who would prefer a more orderly and predictable system, where you could say and prove that certain things are true, and that their opposites are false. Is this so much to ask? Paradox doesn't always work for me (okay, never), even though I believe both that we are doomed and that life is a magical, mystical gift. I love it here, love my life, though sometimes it has been devastating and sometimes, politically, a nightmare.

Life is taxing enough at its most predictable, but you can't bank on *anything*. For example, we learned as children that light is particles, and in a predictable world we would all still agree that since light obviously is particles, like grains of sand, we could all get on with our lives and maybe get the cat a flea dip later. But then you have annoying people who say and can prove that light is also waves, like undulations of water.

The paradox is that both of these are true and they're both true at the same time.

But if both aspects of light are true, then why have they never been observed together in the same room at the same time? (The old Batman/Bruce Wayne question.) If it were left to me, one camp would just give in and say, "Okay, light is particles," or "Fine, have it your way, light is waves."

Maybe life and light are both like that, two mints in one.

How is thinking about this at all helpful to

my tiny princess self? It's disorienting, like a disturbance in the inner ear. So what if the only constant is change? Why bother touching up your roots? What if Mother Teresa was right that "if you love until it hurts, there can be no more hurt, only more love"? Ix-nay on the urt-hay. I have hurt plenty; I'm good on hurt.

Almost every facet of my meager maturation and spiritual understanding has sprung from hurt, loss, and disaster. If it is true that the more you give, the richer you are, would you like my address? Is being born a death sentence—are we, as Beckett said, born astride the grave? If we are born to eternal life, did we already have the good parts that were in process before we existed, where possibly they served dessert with breakfast? These are the questions that keep me up at night.

Paradox means you have to be able to keep two wildly different ideas in your head at the same time. This is one too many for some people, including me on bad days, and sometimes our fearless leaders. I prefer bumper stickers. I really do. "If you lived in your heart, you'd be home now" is all I need as a life philosophy, as I barely avoid smashing into the host bumper it is pasted onto.

But all truth really is paradox, and this turns out to be a reason for hope. If you arrive at a place in life that is miserable, it will change, and something else about it will also be true. So paradox is an invitation to go deeper into life, to see a bigger screen, instead of the nice, safe lower left quadrant where you see work, home, and the country. Try a wider reality, through curiosity, awareness, and breath. Try actually *being* here. What a concept.

The medieval German mystic Meister Eckhart said that if the soul could have known God without the world, God never would have created the world. Paradox is an invitation to know the soul of your own cranky stubborn baby self, and of the sublime. One of the passengers on the famous US Airways Flight 1549 that crash-landed on the Hudson River in 2009 was asked afterward how he felt, and he said, "I was alive before, but now I'm really alive." This is the invitation.

Jesus was a rabbi, schooled by rabbis, who thought like rabbis. Rabbis, upon being asked a question by a disciple, usually answer with a par-adoxical inquiry or a story. This can be annoying and time-consuming for those of us looking for neat, simple answers. But truth is too wild and complex to be contained in one answer, so Jesus often responded with a question or a parable.

Most parables are paradoxical in that they don't go the ways you think they will. Jesus is messing with people's minds, paradoxically out of love, so they dig deeper into truth, where they may find themselves, and love, which is the kingdom.

Take any of Jesus' parables. There's the one about a vineyard owner who goes out all day and hires people, each for the standard daily wage, no matter how many hours they work. At quitting time, he gives the last ones hired the daily wage; but then he also gives the people who've worked the longest the same wage. Of course those who've worked the longest kvetch up a storm. I would have. I'd definitely be bitter. Here's the paradox: The owner notes that each of them got what they'd been promised, i.e., enough, the standard daily wage. Why would anybody—like, say, an addict—want more than enough?

No one you know, I'm sure.

Each of us wants so much assurance, and there really isn't much. We religious types think God's love, closeness, and grace are the answers to all of life's pain and general horribleness. But then something bad happens to our children or our health. A young sober woman of my acquaintance who survived a grueling battle with oral cancer, losing part of her tongue in the process, had been in remission for a couple of years and then shared in a gathering that the cancer had returned. She would need more chemo. Everyone began the litany of stunned encouragement, of knowing someone's aunt's beautician who'd had the same prognosis and was still alive, but the young woman waved it all away like smoke.

"Oh, God's got it," she said cheerfully. I wear these words on a necklace. I believe this with all my heart, but at the same time I also believe in science and chemo.

I once saw on YouTube a home movie of a five-year-old girl sobbing beside her baby brother, who is sitting up with the slight rolling motion of an inflatable Bop clown. She alternately sobs to the camera that she doesn't want him to get older, then stops to cuddle him, gazing at him like a suitor and voicing tenderly that she loves him so much, he is the most precious baby in the world, then sobs to the camera that she doesn't want to die when she's a hundred, then cuddles him and gushes that she loves his little smiles. I think this pretty much says it. We are consumed by the most intense love for one another and the joy of living, along with the grief and terror that we and our babies will know unbelievable hurt: broken bones, bad boyfriends, old age.

We live one day at a time, knowing it's over too soon, in what feels like about eighteen years, seven months. *Zzzzzzzip.* Time for a nice catheter and heart pills. Every day we're in the grip of the impossible conundrum: the truth that it's over in a blink, and we may be near the end, *and* that we have to live as if it's going to be okay, no matter what. Niels Bohr wrote, "The opposite of a true statement is a false statement, but the opposite of a profound truth can be another profound truth."

We think we know what we know, and we love this so much, no matter what Socrates thought. We like to think we stand on the truth, that the ground beneath our feet is stable, moored, which totally works for me. But is it? In the San Francisco Bay Area? Really?

Yet the blessing of knowing that you don't know is to get gently busted. We may not actually want to know this, but we don't have a choice. It is the same feeling when I hit the wrong button on my phone and all the app icons wiggle and jiggle concurrently in what some of us more inept, possibly older people experience as taunting. Entering into paradox, and thus mystery, can be just as overwhelming. But this is also where new beginnings and hope emerge, side by side with the dark and scrambled.

Some characters in fiction and our families exist as levers, to turn everything upside down and thereby knock out of the park some of our old presumptions, pretensions, convictions, and illusions of safety. These people, both in fiction and at the holiday table, tend to be annoying and on the margins. No one is touching their hems. Just the opposite, in fact. We laugh at them, roll our eyes inwardly, and try to figure out a way not to have to sit next to them.

Someone with whom I was in love felt it made sense to criticize my son to me, to Armed Tense Mother Bear, over the phone, unsolicited and in great detail, out of the blue, and express judgment about his character and parenting. My reaction was instant, weaponized love for my son—and so I withheld from this person my affection and the invitation to my heart, let alone my bed. Forget letting go and letting God. It was time for brooding, stewing, victimized self-righteousness, and thoughts of revenge. Now you're talking.

I told him coldly, "You've hurt me, and our whole family, by having these bad secret judgments all along. You've sullied us, and our home."

First he tried to explain that I was misinterpreting his attack on my son, as he really wanted to help him become a better father. This is a wonderful and honest man, but I didn't buy it, and I said so.

He asked what I thought he should do. I said, with decades of therapy and church behind me, that there was *nothing* he could do. Ever.

He went off to think this over. The next day, he asked me again.

I said, "You need to make this right." And he agreed to do that.

I prayed and cried and came to sort of believe that he was perfect and also an asshat, and that I am, too. Then the next day, when he came over to talk, I was packing heat. We spoke for a few minutes, although I didn't feel like talking, but in a crazy subconscious martial arts move, God or Holy Spirit or Coyote Trickster intervened and I found myself inviting him along to Home Depot, where I had some errands to do. Home Depot, where they fix things and make things right.

He came along, and he began to make things right by listening, finding in himself the willingness to look at his own stuff, and change, at my house, with my son.

Since then, we love and trust each other more than we already did.

When we are stuck in our convictions and personas, we enter into the disease of having good ideas and being right. My Jesuit friend Tom used to say that he never noticed what he was feeling; only that he was right. We think we have a lock on truth, with our burnished surfaces and articulation, but the bigger we pump ourselves up, the easier we are to prick with a pin. And the bigger we get, the harder it is to see the earth under our feet.

We all know the horror of having been Right with a capital R, feeling the surge of a cause, whether in politics or custody disputes. This rightness is so hot and steamy and exciting, until the inevitable rug gets pulled out from under us. Then we get to see that we almost never really know what is true, except what everybody else knows: that sometimes we're all really lonely, and hollow, and stripped down to our most naked human selves.

It is the worst thing on earth, this truth about how little truth we know. I hate and resent it. And yet it is where new life rises from.

New life is uncomfortable, nubbly. We like

soft and warm. Baby blankets are nice. We also like to wear the fleecy cloak we've made for ourselves, the finery of being right.

Why would you take off the cloak voluntarily? It's so comfortable and impressive, at least to you. You let it drop or life yanks it off, and when you notice it's gone, it doesn't feel great. You begin to feel the cold, prickly wind, and people can see your veiny ankles.

But what comes in is fresh air on our skin, which startles us awake. We'll never again be as open and vibrational as babies, but maybe now we'll be a little more present and aware.

The forty-three people who died in the catastrophic fires in Santa Rosa, California, in 2017 lost everything. The survivors lost almost as much: their homes, gardens, friends, property, pets. But they had one another. They had life. And they had us—shabby, busy us. The fire was a sword that cut away all the comfort and treasure in life, the illusion of the solidity of objects, which turns out not to be so solid after all.

We saw devastation, of course, but we also witnessed holiness in the burned world and what was left standing—a fireplace, a heavily laden persimmon tree, pallets of bottled water from out of state, the sky. We saw humanity.

Don't get me wrong—it sucked. I believe I would grieve and wail forever if this happened to me. But I would be mistaken. I would come through, via friends, community, love, grace, relief efforts. We are flattened, we come through.

Usually this holiness takes a backseat to our toxic self-obsessed nattering monkey minds. But in the Wine Country, when so much was burned and chopped away, when people's hearts pounded with fear, when their breath constricted with loss, there was another heart beating with them— ours. Another breath was with them, and there were hands to hold. Such beautiful comfort, the holy form, the only comfort there really is—the heart, a breath, a hand. It is not the comfort I would choose, but the survivors found themselves surrounded with solace, with food, clothing, art supplies for their kids. (And sports bras! Relief organizations asked for new sports bras, instead of our armpitty discards, which many women were donating with good intentions. My son bought $200 worth of sports bras. Try explaining that to your accountant.) The survivors were alive, and aliveness is sacred.

That is the paradox, that aliveness is chemical, electrical, and sacred. Aliveness is what we find way deep down inside, for a moment here, an interval there, those pulses that go on inside us all the time, in our homes, in our environment, and in the universe, the continuum from which we are so often isolated in our self-conscious kiosks, by habit and upbringing. The moment is truth, and so is the continuum.

Scientists say we are made of stars, and I believe them, although my upper arms look like hell. Maybe someday the stars will reabsorb me. Maybe, as fundamentalist Christians have shared with me, I will rot in hell for all eternity, which I would hate, because I am very sensitive. Besides, I have known hell, and I have also known love. Love was bigger.

What comforts us is that, after we make ourselves crazy enough, we can let go inch by inch into just being here; every so often, briefly. There is flow everywhere in nature—glaciers are just rivers that are moving really, really slowly—so how could there not be flow in each of us? Or at least in most of us? When we detach or are detached by tragedy or choice from the tendrils of identity, unexpected elements feed us. There is weird food in the flow, like the wiggly bits that birds watch for in tidal channels. Protein and greens are obvious food, but so is buoyancy, when we don't feel as mired in the silt of despair.

Our lives bob along on the sea of ordinariness, turmoil, paperwhites about to bloom, matters of state, war about to be waged, although when has it ever, even once, led to the predicted consequences? As we grow older, we know what is always there in the wings, some of it not very good news. Then it's here, and it may be as awful as we'd imagined, as in the Santa Rosa fires, or just as stunning, as in the response.

How can we celebrate paradox, let alone manage at all, knowing how scary the future may be—that the baby brother will grow, and ignore you or hurt you or break your heart? Or that we may die, after an unattractive decline, or bomb North Korea later today? We remember that because truth is paradox, something beautiful is also going on. So while trusting that and waiting for revelation, we do the next right thing. We tell the truth. We march, make dinner, have rummage sales to raise relief funds. Whoever arranges such things keeps distracting us and shifting things around so we don't get stuck in hopelessness: we can take one loud, sucking, disengaging step back into hope. We remember mustard seeds, that the littlest things will have great results. We do the smallest, realest, most human things. We water that which is dry.

TWO

Inside Job

There is almost nothing outside you that will help in any kind of lasting way, unless you are waiting for a donor organ. You can't buy, achieve, or date serenity. Peace of mind is an inside job, unrelated to fame, fortune, or whether your partner loves you. Horribly, what this means is that it is also an inside job for the few people you love most desperately in the world. We cannot arrange lasting safety or happiness for our most beloved people. They have to find their own ways, their own answers.

Not one single person in history has gotten an alcoholic sober. (Maybe you'll be the first.

But—and I say this with love—I doubt it.) If it is someone else's problem, you probably don't have the solution.

I hate this. I have my eye on a new rug for my study that would so inspire me to write better, faster, smarter. Also, on some leftover Halloween candy, which I know this one time wouldn't give me a sugar rush and the inevitable crash. And I have a list of excellent ideas on how almost everyone I know should proceed in order to improve the quality of their lives, which might coincidentally improve the quality of mine, as I could stop worrying about their bad choices and wasted potential.

The desperate drive to own and control in order to fill our psychic holes, relieve anxiety, fix difficulties, and cauterize old wounds takes root at an early age, and is doomed. It is like going to the hardware store for bread. It doesn't sell bread. I can live on corn nuts and Paydays for only so long. Probably no longer than two weeks.

Maybe retracing our steps to the origin of the problem is helpful. Most emotional wounds are caused by a child's belief or feedback that he is deficient, defective, or annoying—probably all three. Perhaps the father had tiny warmth issues, and the mother was a bit tense, or vice versa. To make the parents proud, the child needed to do better, add certain qualities, gain or lose some weight, remove any offending traits or tics, and not make other people get inferiority complexes.

Some of us felt like walking tics, too sensitive or rebellious, needy or robotic—damaged like an air conditioner that was dropped in the warehouse, and when the worker points out that it's broken the boss says: "Just put it in a new box. Ship it out."

The message to us kids was that we didn't have intrinsic value but we could earn it, and that we lived in a world of scarcity but just needed new things. We were simultaneously disappointing and better than people in other families. Evil outweighed good, scarcity outweighed care and abundance. So stay on your toes, but why, for Chrissakes, are you such a nervous Nellie?

Two tactics helped. Putting together a reasonably good personality was how we staked a claim on the outside world, although it meant ignoring our inside world. That personality needed to be one that succeeded—so those participation medals were almost as damaging as first-place trophies. You got a pat on the head.

And the other tactic was to achieve enough to hoard better and better stuff that most people couldn't even afford.

This was life in the hardware store, and just fine if you could live on beef snack sticks and Beer Nuts. Dad was under enough pressure as it was without your looking so pitiful; heavy and distracted lies the head that wears the crown.

The bakery, on the other hand, was a family's understanding that a kid didn't have to do or achieve or own anything more for the world to care, and even delight in her. One met families like this from time to time (not very many— maybe one a year). How did the rest of us ever locate a spiritual bakery where we could actually find the bread of life, let alone the ginger cookies of hope? The answer is, over the years, little by little, mosaic chip by mosaic chip.

I heard something a few years ago that would have completely changed my life had I learned it as a child. It was at my church, where I was teaching my Sunday school class of two teenage boys, both with rough skin, one slightly younger boy, and a little girl with elaborate and charming buckteeth, too young for braces. That day I was teaching my one good message, that we are loved and chosen as is, fearfully and wonderfully made, with love and awe, perfect and fragile. We are lovely as sparrows, and all sparrows are sweet. No one thinks, "That sparrow is kind of a loser, and boy, is that one letting herself go."

I know that all teenagers believe they are intrinsically defective, so that was why I brought up sparrows and friends. I asked the class if any of their best friends had acne, glasses, or problems at home, and if that made them love the friends less. Of course not. I asked them to say, "I have value," and both teenagers did so with mortification. The younger boy, not yet destroyed by hormones and society, said it as calmly as if announcing he had ears.

I turned to the little girl, expectantly. She said, "I has value!"

I asked her to say it again, "I has value."

I has value. I want to get that tattooed on my forearm.

Besides extreme achievement, basic jungle-survival growing up meant agreeing not to see what was going on in the family but also agreeing to feel responsible for the parents' unhappiness. Maybe there were tiny, tiny flaws and tensions in the marriage, such as that the parents hated each other, or that the father was a sociopath. Love did not look like family unity, it looked like a business arrangement between mom, dad, and the serfs. It looked like kids trying to fix unhappy parents by being successful, having good manners, and making handmade cards—#1 Mom! Underachievement and precociousness both sped up the feeling of separation. If you were going to get ahead, you needed a strategy, a charming persona. Imagination and heartfulness were distracting.

Who knows, maybe this all begins prenatally. Looking back on it, I'm not convinced that my parents' smoking and drinking and bad marriage produced an ideal environment for a possibly already tense fetus. By kindergarten, I knew I had more value when I cheered up my parents, did well in school, and finished my chores. In the 1950s, little girls baked and learned to dust furniture, and this pleased everyone—briefly. When I was needy, shy, worried, deeply sensitive, too skinny or, later, overweight—in other words, most *me*—not so much.

As you grew, you collected possessions, the psychic kind you needed to survive: the armor to ward off emotional battery; the snippets of good advice ("Never let them see you cry") you picked up as you grew. You needed to guard these possessions, and what better safe-deposit box than your body? Plenty of room next to the family secrets and all the scary feelings you swallowed.

Finally, in high school or college, you met someone who knew something deeper, true and ineffable. They gave you poems and wine. That was the medicine, the food, the knowledge of essence—yours and the world's—and belonging. When we discovered who we truly are, through love or a teacher, new life began. We discovered, now and then, our inclusion in the huge, beautiful, weird world, in new friends, communities, the most ordinary elements: we break the bread, bless the cup, and share.

Even so, after finding those friends and those poems, and maybe even coming to believe that the world is tilted to the good, our default response still is the child's drive to be more accomplished, to be attractive and self-sufficient, with a better class of friends.

Forty-four years after I dropped out of college, despite decades of extraordinary friends, spirituality, and (some) mental healing that I've managed to accumulate along the way, my first response to hearing the number of people killed so far in the Syrian genocide was to do the single most bourgeois thing my unconscious mind could come up with: drive to Nordstrom for a $200 pair of jeans that I'd coveted. Two hundred dollars, and I didn't even look that cute in them.

When my perfect dog Sadie died fifteen years ago, I bought the first new car of my life a week later, a soft minty-green VW bug. God told me to, and it helped for a few days. When a large newspaper's book critic panned my previous book, saying it seemed to have been written by someone who was spending too much time with the Kardashians, I felt humiliated. The paper has 500,000 readers. How to deal with this? A Cinnabon is a thing of perfection, and the extra frosting costs only 71 cents.

A child said to me, "I has value," but the grown-ups mostly keep that thought to themselves, and I keep forgetting that I do.

Could you say this about yourself right now, that you have immense and intrinsic value, at your current weight and income level, while waiting to hear if you got the job or didn't, or sold your book or didn't?

This idea that I had all the value I'd ever need was concealed from me my whole life. I want a refund. In this world of suffering and grace, of brokenness and sky, of bad skin and buckteeth and one another, I cannot add to the value of myself. It's not out there.

This poses the question: If it's not out there for sale or to achieve, then where is it?

It's everywhere, within and without, around and above, in the most ordinary and trivial, in bread and roses, a glass of water, in dawn and midnight. All you have to do is want to see. You still get to hang on to your own strategies, cravings, peccadilloes, ambition, your $200 jeans and your DKNY cashmere coat of mail. You can still have ice cream, but maybe now you don't need Bourbon Fig Butter Gelato with Unborn Pistachios. And maybe you can taste each bite, and not have to shovel it in like a backhoe.

(Maybe you do. Sometimes one just does, and there is nothing wrong with this.)

It's all here, everything we seek and need, inside us. This does not mean that I don't daydream about the latest iPhone or Tesla, or try to fix a struggling relative. But it won't work for any length of time. Then there I'll be, in my superior clutter, bookshelves groaning with tomes that surely set me apart as an intellect, with a phone I can't work. And the same old existential dread.

I absolutely don't buy into the current mania for tidiness and decluttering. For a writer, piles of papers and notes are a fertile field. Keep all those books you read in college, or had certainly meant to read. Keep all those clothes that last fit during the Carter administration. Or give them away. It's for you to choose. You has value.

This is a great awakening, but with it comes horrible news: Everyone else has value, too. Even the horrible relatives you can't stand. And the ones in your family who are over the age of eighteen are exactly where they are supposed to be, or at least get to be. They has value, as they are, whether heroic or appalling.

Heroic is better, of course, because people compliment you on what a great parenting job you did, and you get to (briefly) have better self-esteem and worry less about your children's mortality.

Appalling is harder because of the natural fixation that you can rescue your kids, and ought to. Your good ideas for them would certainly straighten them out and help them make healthier choices. These would help you enjoy life more, too, so what's the harm in your little suggestions, demands, funding?

The harm is in the unwanted help or helping them when they need to figure things out for themselves. Help is the sunny side of control.

There is nothing outside them, nothing they can date, buy, or achieve, that will fill the hole inside them or help them hit the reset button. But it's very productive of you to try, and try, and try, although they tend to get sicker, as do you. Plus, they start to hate you. So there's that.

From an early age in chaotic, confusing families, another survival instinct was to try to get more information about everything, especially about how all the adults were doing, and how things were going to turn out. (This is still my first response to deep anxiety.) We needed to figure things out. This would surely make things less worrisome. At sixteen, all we needed was our driver's license and a girlfriend or boyfriend. Later, all we needed was a job. That was the carrot, the dream, what we needed; it was attainable, almost within reach. Christians say that whatever you think you need to be happy is where the devil will get in. In recovery, we might say that this is where your disease will attack you.

Jung wrote that when we look outside ourselves, we dream. When we look inside, we wake up. Why would you walk out of a lovely dream, or Plato's cave, into real life?

One answer is that life lasts so briefly, like free theater in the park—glorious and tedious; full of wonder and often hard to understand, but right before our very eyes, and capable of rousing us, awakening us to life, to the bright green and very real grass, the mess, the sky, the limbo. This is the great unexpected promise, that we can choose now, no matter our current condition. But we can't choose it for anyone else.

You can raise and care for your nearest and dearest the best you can, put them in the best schools, rehab, condo, or memory care, and never, ever give up on their having the best possible life available. But if you do so thinking you can rescue them with your good ideas and your checkbook, or get them to choose a healthy, realistic way of life, that mistake will make both of you much worse than you already are.

My lifelong and core belief, right after the conviction that I was defective, mildly annoying, and better than everyone else, was that my help was helpful. I began trying to save my parents almost before I could speak, with goodness, helpfulness, and precocity. It did not go all that well. Their elevator was going only one way: down. Because I couldn't change that, it separated me from myself.

Next I tried to save my brothers from how unwell my parents insisted on staying, using my life force and good ideas to this end. This proved just as disappointing. My brothers followed their own disastrous paths, breaking my heart.

Next I decided I could rescue my best friends and boyfriends, usually while the friends and boyfriends were trying to fix *me*. I bought them things and provided services that would cheer them up, and if I did not fix them, then I tried to give them a fix. But there is no fix.

My older brother, John, was the first person to break free of my helpful relief efforts. He surrendered and began to recover. He initially came to me one night for help, as everyone in the family always had done, on his first day of not drinking or using. He looked scared to death, like a handsome wino whose old dog had just died.

My best thought was to offer him a cool re-freshing beer.

I just wanted to save him—from his pain, his self-loathing, his physical decline, and his abso-lute utter desperation. I was not yet familiar with what the phrase "the bottom" meant, although I did know firsthand and from art about the dark night of the soul. My brother was there, I could tell, and I thought he needed a beer. Nor did I know about grace, that it meets you exactly where you are, at your most pathetic and hopeless, and it loads you into its wheelbarrow and then tips you out somewhere else in ever so slightly better shape.

He turned down the beer and said he needed help. He was crying. If we are lucky, hitting bot-tom includes this. He wanted me to take a Pola-roid of him so he'd never forget this. Then through some honest-to-God miracle I said the words "Call Jack"—an older sober family friend. He did.

That night Jack, and later some other local sober guys, took John under their great collective wing, a wing with warm mussed feathers, neck tattoos, and bad coffee. Neither my brother nor they needed anything from me except for me to get out of John's way, and release him.

That was thirty-five years ago.

There was no way I could have predicted that a few years later, I, too, would call Jack, and five months later, our younger brother would, too. And I couldn't have known that years later I would see my precious, amazing, twenty-two-year-old son in the same shape as my brother in that Polaroid: handsome wino, dead dog.

What did I do? My default setting was to set about saving him from himself, fixing him.

That went well. I had to spend tens of thousands of dollars and a hundred sleepless nights until I, too, hit a bottom.

Grace helped me throw in the towel. Or rather it helped pry it out of my cold, dead hands. I got help—for me. I stopped routinely giving my son money and a place to sleep. I accepted that he might end up dead and that I absolutely could not save him. It was the very, very worst time of my life.

A community of like parents stepped in. Eventually I was able to leave him in jail when he got arrested.

People without scary kids gaped at me and asked, "You did *what?*"

People with scary kids who had not yet hit bottom gaped at me and asked where I had found the strength. The answer is simple. I found the strength in the old formula of failure, terror, impotence, and grace, the terror that if I fished my kid out again, this person I had loved far more than anyone else on earth would die. I had gotten him an apartment, a good used truck, a credit card, and I could see he was worse.

"But that is so extreme!" people said. "Jail is dangerous, and so cold."

"Wow," I said. "Bummer."

His life was just as cold and dangerous, and I believe to this day that if I had bailed him out, he would not still be here on this earth, in the other room playing Lego Minecraft with his son. I only know that on September 13, 2011, he called me to say he had had a week clean and sober.

As I write this, that was six years ago—six

years and two months. Not that I fixate on his program, but six years, two months, two days, and three hours.

It was an inside job, with a lot of friends who were named Not His Mother, men who got to stay sober by helping newcomers. They helped him so they would stay sober and so that he could help newcomers, too, down the road. (Trust me, they are everywhere.) He called them when he was suffering, instead of his darling helpful mother, who accepted that she had her own inside job and community. I released him (mostly) and surrendered.

I practiced all the Gets I could think of: I got off of that poor guy's back. I got out of his way, so I didn't block the connection or energy between him and his higher power, whom he calls The Muffin. I got right with my own sense of God, and eventually I became a recovering higher power. I got on with my own life, which is blessed beyond words and sometimes frustrating.

I still sometimes shop or binge, but it doesn't help any more than it ever did—i.e., briefly, and with a hangover. So I practice the fifth Get: I get in touch with others. I tell my partner the truth about how crunchy I feel inside, how unevolved or vindictive. Or I pick up the three-hundred-pound phone and tell a close friend. Or I get in the car and head to where one of my precious communities has gathered. This might be a park, my church, my Sunday school room; with hikers, sober people, townsfolk. You show up as is, hangdog, skeptical, pissy, or superior. Someone welcomes you and pats the seat next to them. Someone will get other people water, or watch the kids, or do a neighbor's laundry, or wash somebody's feet.

THREE

Humans 101

Almost everyone is screwed up, broken, clingy, scared, and yet designed for joy. Even (or especially) people who seem to have it more or less together are more like the rest of us than you would believe. I try not to compare my insides to their outsides, because this makes me much worse than I already am, and if I get to know them, they turn out to have plenty of irritability and shadow of their own. Besides, those few people who aren't a mess are probably good for about twenty minutes of dinner conversation.

This is good news, that almost everyone is petty, narcissistic, secretly insecure, and in it for themselves, because a few of the funny ones may actually long to be friends with you and me. They can be real with us, the greatest relief.

As we develop love, appreciation, and forgiveness for others over time, we may accidentally develop those things toward ourselves, too. While you might think it's a trick, having affection for one's goofy, crabby, annoying, lovely self is home. This has been my meager salvation.

That we are designed for joy is exhilarating, within reach, now or perhaps later today, after a nap, as long as we do not mistake excitement for joy. Joy is good cheer. My partner says joy and curiosity are the same thing. Joy is always a surprise, and often a decision.

Joy is portable. Joy is a habit, and these days, it can be a radical act. Buffy Sainte-Marie said, "Keep your nose to the joy trail." So for now let's define joy as a slightly giddy appreciation, an inquisitive stirring, as when you see the first crocuses, the earliest struggling, stunted emergence of color in late winter, cream or gold against the tans and browns.

To have a few amazing friends on this side of

eternity, this sometimes grotesque amusement park, is the greatest joy. As Saint Bette sang in the bathhouses, "You got to have friends." We cannot depend solely on spouses to dump on, to share our intimate thoughts with or reveal our deepest truths to. Trust me, they have been through enough just living with us. Our yokes are heavy. Healthy people need to unburden sometimes unpleasant feelings and information, such as hating everything about life and everyone on earth, and hoping the bad people are killed by snakes; or that they just ate all the frosting off a Safeway carrot cake because they were feeling fragile.

It is very normal—and in fact, increasingly so—for anyone in their right mind to feel or do these things, and so therapeutic to tell the miserable truth.

Everyone is capable of making at least one friend, even the worst of your relatives or the crabby neighbor down the street. We all know someone who is really pretty awful in every way yet who has managed to find a loyal friend or two. And then there are the ostentatious displays of this. Maybe your sad widowed uncle, who is angry and heavy-footed and who doesn't even pretend to care to be interested in others at the holiday table, has a devoted friend, his own Bebe Rebozo, and even finds a girlfriend in late life, in a bar, church, convalescent home. His default assumption is that the world is mean and you need to stand up to it with suspicion fueled by fury. Don't put your weapons down for a minute, because then they'll get you, he'll say, and he doesn't even bother covering up what's deep inside him and most of us: fear and greed and laziness. Mine Mine Mine. Then he shows up one miraculous day with a very sweet girlfriend, and at their cheapskate wedding when they dance, he holds her delicately. In their little circle of privacy, this is his sacred ground.

This is how most of us are—stripped down to the bone, living along a thin sliver of what we can bear and control, until life or a friend or disaster nudges us into baby steps of expansion. We're all both irritating and a comfort, our insides both hard and gentle, our hearts both atrophied and pure.

How did we all get so screwed up? Putting

aside our damaged parents, poverty, abuse, addiction, disease, and other unpleasantries, life just damages people. There is no way around this. Not all the glitter and concealer in the world can cover it up. We may have been raised in the illusion that if we played our cards right, life would work out. But it didn't, it doesn't.

This is very disappointing. What a betrayal. They *said*.

It was worse in almost every practical way in medieval times, but some things then were categorically true—everyone just died, the food was dirty, all rulers were evil, you didn't expect too much. You could bank on this.

But with antibiotics and technology came great expectations, of being able to keep our children safe, of living long and healthy lives, relaxed and content and able to keep up the car payments. Even with the Internet, deciphering the genetic code, and great advances in immunotherapy, life is frequently confusing at best, and guaranteed to be hard and weird and sad at times. These days things are about as mortally coiled as they can be, our young as vulnerable as chicks, our old just as stunningly decrepit as in medieval times but now living forever.

We witness and try to alleviate others' suffering, but sometimes it just outdoes itself and we are left gasping, groaning. And running through it all there is the jangle, both the machines outside and the chattering treeful of monkeys inside us.

We believe that we are all in this together; this was the message of childhood, that being together meant connection, like an electrical circuit—think school recess on the blacktop, summer camp, and all those family holiday gatherings. Ram Dass said that if you think you're enlightened, go spend a week with your family. With our nearest and dearest gathered together, we sometimes intuit that they are neither nearest nor dearest. No one is speaking to Great-Aunt Elaine, who voted for and is still stumping for Ted Cruz. Your mom or dad (you can't remember which) had an emotional affair with the office manager, or the older cousins had done unforgivable things to the younger ones, or there was nothing overt but everyone sort of hated everyone else. Pass the gravy, Phil!

The nature of our basic family dysfunction is that we want to present to the world as a kindly, engaged, smart clan that's doing just fine. (In recovery, we call fine "Fucked-up, Insecure, Neurotic, and Emotional.") But underneath, we have resentment, fear for our children, and an addictive desperation to check our texts. There may also be an irregular mole on your thigh that pulses with death, and unexplained bruising.

There's just no way around this. Even when life sorts itself out and starts to work and we revel in what is working, the cosmic banana peel awaits. Without this reality, there would be no great art or comedy.

So we savor what works when things are sort of harmonious. You almost stubbed your toe on the way to the shed, but you didn't. Nelson Mandela got out of prison. The mole is just an inflamed keratosis. Your child finally checked in. The sun and a lemon soufflé both rose. These are fleeting, lovely satisfactions.

Granted, these moments are not exactly the music of the spheres, but if there is enough money this month to buy new tires for the car, and if no country blew up any other country while you slept, and the food actually tastes pretty good and is not dirty? Dibs. It gives us a baseline hope.

And there is always nature, her royal self, who offers herself both as a light show and as bread to be eaten. We hang with her as much as possible, because nature really knows how to do it when she is not being mercurial and destroying entire regions. We do get a taste of the spheres in birdsong, eclipses, the surf, tangerines. In the dark, we see the stars. In the aftermath of the devastating fire, the sun rose red.

To pay close attention to and mostly accept your life, inside and out and around your body, is to be halfway home. An old woman in twelve-step recovery once told me that while there is an elaborate prayer in one of the steps, of turning one's life and all results over to the care of God, as each person understands God, she and some of the old-timers secretly pray upon waking, "Whatever," and pray before falling asleep, "Oh, well."

The lesson here is that there is no fix. There is, however, forgiveness. To forgive yourselves and others constantly is necessary. Not only is everyone screwed up, but everyone screws up.

How can we know all this, yet somehow experience joy? Because that's how we're designed— for awareness and curiosity. We are hardwired with curiosity inside us, because life knew that this would keep us going even in bad sailing. We see the newborn energy of the universe most flagrantly in the sea and in the entire Jell-O-y wiggle of a baby. The universe expresses itself most showily as children, and it moves through children of all ages—your nephew, baby Jesus, and Ruth Gordon in *Harold and Maude*, shimmying at eighty in a cocktail dress. Life feeds anyone who is open to taste its food, wonder, and glee— its immediacy. We see this toward the end of many people's lives, when everything in their wasted bodies fights to stay alive, for a few more kisses or bites of ice cream, one more hour with you. Life is still flowing through them: life *is* them.

Take children with very little, and the joy of their nightly bath, the play and the purity; the combing of a toy horse's mane, the brushing of a favorite doll's hair; fitting things together. Little kids sharing a mayonnaise sandwich, making fart noises and speaking fake foreign languages, becoming robots and jungle animals, creating futures out of half-deflated soccer balls, magic and hilarity out of absolutely anything. We see the pleasure of the man with Lou Gehrig's disease in a wheelchair at the baseball park with his wife on a warm clear night. The freshets of joy when things temporarily work: the senses, the muscles, the mind. We start with that freshness, which cannot be created or destroyed. That's magic, or the human spirit, or hope—whatever you want to call it—to captivate, to share contented time.

Some of us periodically need to repeat the joy training, rehabilitate the part of us that naturally dims or gets injured by busyness, or just by too much bad news to bear. Adults rarely have the imagination or energy of children, but we do have one another, and nature, and old black-and-white movies, and the ultimate secret weapon, books. Books! To fling myself into a book, to be carried away to another world while being at my most grounded, on my butt or in my bed or favorite chair, is literally how I have survived being here at all. Someone else is doing the living for me, and all I have to do is let their stories, humor, knowledge, and images—some of which I'll never forget—flow through me, even as I forget to turn off the car when I arrive at my destination. I remember lines from *A Wrinkle in Time* from fifty-five years ago: "Only a fool is not afraid." Even as I sometimes go out in shoes that don't match, I remember L'Engle's words, "Believing takes practice." Plopped in my chair, I get to be elsewhere, immersed in humanity, exclaiming in silence, "Yes, that's just the way it is," or "Thank God it's not that way for me." I get taken out of myself, and I get to salute all the people and experiences I recognize, with surprise and pleasure. "I *so* get that, but I never found the words. I know her. I *am* her." This reactivates the giddiness muscle, and giddiness leaves you almost no choice but to share, and sharing is what makes us happy.

What other than books is inside me or nearby that can help connect with what has meaning? Prayer? Breath? Movement? Oranges? Cats? What about staring at the night sky? What about getting to a window and looking out with the attention and curiosity we see in little kids? I'll do it for you this one time. Winter is almost here, so it is not exactly Versailles outside, but the earth outside my window is patched with green sprouts amid brown patches of dirt and fallen gold. The soil looks tough and lumpy. Ants walk the length of grass planks and a couple of sow bugs move together slowly over an orange leaf in a spot of damp soil. Unlike roly-polies, which can roll up for protection like tiny armadillos, sow bugs can't roll. And they are not really bugs, but land-living crustaceans, like crabs or lobsters, that breathe through gills. Isn't that wild? The tufts of grass are more green than brown, which surprises me. Wow: there must have been more moisture in the air and earth than I'd thought.

Unplugged

Almost everything will work again if you unplug it for a few minutes, including you.

Don't Let Them Get You to Hate Them

How did we become so filled with hate? This is not who we are. Hate is the worst emotion of all, second only to acute jealousy.

Certain special people of late have caused a majority of us to experience derangement. Some of us have developed hunchbacks, or tics in our eyelids. Even my Buddhist friends have been feeling despair, and when they go bad, you know the end is nigh. Booker T. Washington said, "I shall allow no man to belittle my soul by making me hate him," and this is the most awful thing about it. Yet part of me sort of likes it, too, for the flush of righteousness, the bond to half of the electorate. Who would we be without hate? In politics, breakups, custody disputes, hate turns us into them, with a hangover to boot, the brown-bottle flu of the spirit.

Hate is such an ugly word. How about *loathe* for the verb, *abhorrence* for the noun?

A friend once said that at the end of his drinking, he was deteriorating faster than he could lower his standards, and this began happening to me recently with hate. Some of my wise, more evolved friends say that loathing certain people, henceforth referred to as Them, is not worth the effort, that they are too thin as human forms to actually hate. I say, "Not for me, baby." Others remind us they are all children of God, loved just as deeply as my grandson.

I say, That is very nice.

Hate, on the one hand, is comforting, but regrettably, on the other, it's malignant. I loathe certain public individuals with great wriggling discomfort, and it steadies me. It's not white-hot hate, as I can't afford to be ignited and let it consume my life, but there is a lot of heat in there, a combination of sickness and fire. The fever makes me into a war zone of blasts, rubble, mission creep, and the ministrations of my own private USO. It steals me from what one might call my better angels, my higher self, my center; *c'est la guerre.* I have been one of the walking wounded for a year or so—actually more like the zombies in *Night of the Living Dead,* because we are fused with people when we hate them. We're not us anymore. We become like them. They—Them—are really not doing anything to us. To some extent, I am doing it to myself—the zombification is complete. I'm all parts: the host, the carrier, the new victim.

I can't change them. So I pray, Bless them with nice retirement opportunities, and change me, but while You're at it, help them not to blow up the entire world. Thanks.

Has there ever been more hate loosed upon the world than now? Probably. But there didn't use to be as many automatic weapons, as much advanced military firepower, or such efficiency.

Twentieth-century technology allowed the camps to be built. So . . . not ideal. Nowadays many of us feel that the coldest possible wind is blowing, as in a bad snow globe; and every day is worse. As someone said not long ago, it's all Four Horsemen now, all the time.

When I finally got to the point that I couldn't take it anymore, I decided to put down my weapons briefly. Maybe I would end up on the winning side, calmer, or at least less deranged. So as is my habit, I asked God for help with the mess of me. God immediately sent in two people. The first was Martin Luther King, quoted on Twitter, that hate cannot drive out hate, only love can. That sucks. Yet it was enough for me to realize that I needed palliative care. The second was an eight-year-old boy.

I asked one of my Sunday school kids if he believed God was always with him, helping him. He thought about this for a moment and replied, "Maybe forty percent."

Forty percent! What if I could reduce my viral load by forty percent?

Everything good begins with awareness,

whether awakening to the momentousness of the present or to the damage we are causing. In my case, hate is fear and anger at not getting what I want, being afraid of people whose values are so alien to me, and of the unknown. Also, of being blown up. Some of us wake up afraid, and choose our political opposites to be the focus of that fear. We think we have the answers to life's problems—we may need electric cars, windmills, more money, and a few extra atomic weapons. Fear causes fight or flight, but hate alleviates the shame of feeling frozen. Hate is a massive mood-alterer, like a speedball of heroin and cocaine, or at least like sugar: swift, stimulating, toxic.

The willingness to look at and maybe change addictive behavior results only from internal pain, severe hangovers, and public disgrace, the sense of being soiled, inside and out, craving a shower with something rough to scour it all off, like an extra-strength loofah. The courage to change the things we can means the stuff inside the snow globe, not where it sits on the mantel. Of course we hate the corporate evildoers and what they are doing to us and to the earth, assuring a future for our grandchildren that is more horrifying than anything we've lived through. Of course we hate the man who raped our friend or abused our child. And I'm going out on a limb here, but almost everyone hates the spokespeople for the NRA.

Awareness helped me make progress in my evolution, like going from finger paints to potato prints. I began to hear people who busted me. One morning recently at the beginning of her sermon, my pastor cited the same Dr. King quotation I'd just come upon, that hate cannot drive out hate, only love can, and I thought, "I heard it the first time." Then at the end of the sermon, wrapping up, she said, sighing, "Just don't let them get you to hate them."

I have not been the same since. She ruined hate for me.

Of course my first response was like Dana Carvey's Church Lady, "Well! Isn't that special," but the pastor's words really got to me. I shared my experience at lunch not long after with someone whose feelings had led to a ten-pound weight gain and a persistent rash: her hate *showed*. I told her about my project and sucked her into my web; we got into the juiciest discussion about the origins of hate. She said that as a child she'd hated her father for how he treated her mother while he pretended to the world to be such a good guy. And yet she desperately wanted his approval. But he didn't respond to her, and she was left alone with her own shame and self-loathing about wanting to be appreciated by a mean man. It felt like there was domestic violence going on inside her, between the bully and the mother. The conflict left a mucky mess within her, like a cake that wouldn't completely bake, no matter how long you left it in the oven. Without intervention, she turned on herself by feeling ashamed, and she could settle into that, because it was home: bullying, shame, longing.

Of course you would hate any man who made you feel like this. Talking about it that day helped her break out of the cake, like a showgirl.

Everyone with whom I shared my pastor's words experienced something similar. Haters want us to hate them, because hate is incapacitating. When we hate, we can't operate from our real selves, which is our strength. Now that I think of it, this is such a great reason to give up our hate—as revenge, to deprive the haters of what they want.

Some people are able to distance themselves from the people they can't stand by simply not watching the news. Not me. Also, avoiding the news sometimes just suppresses the angry, scared feelings, which can do damage internally, and unconsciously, I had always been more apt to fixate and spew, until recently when the hate started kicking my butt.

Something that helps is to look at adversaries as people who are helping you do a kind of emotional weight training, Nautilus for your character. They may have been assigned to you, to annoy or exhaust you. They are actually caseworkers. When my pastor calls the most difficult, annoying people in her life her grace-builders, I want to jump out the window. I am so not there yet, but I understand what she's talking about.

Awareness spritzes us awake. Being awake means that we have taken off the blinders. We can choose to see or to squinch our eyes shut like a child, which looks silly on people over eighty pounds. Awareness means showing up, availing oneself of the world, so there is the chance that empathy will step up to bat, even in this lifetime. If we work hard and are lucky, we may come to see everyone as precious, struggling souls.

God is better at this than I am.

In my defense, it is my understanding that God is both here and on another, gentler plane, and does not have my sensitive digestive system. Frederick Buechner addresses this: "And then there is the love for the enemy—love for the one who does not love you but mocks, threatens, and inflicts pain. The tortured's love for the torturer. This is God's love. It conquers the world." The book this came from is called *The Magnificent Defeat*, which is about surrender—something else that is a bit of a stretch for me. My secret belief is that if we surrender, then we give up all hope of delaying the effects of our global catastrophe, of creating a world that is less excruciating for children and the poor.

Surrender might have come more naturally to us if we had not had families. I'm just saying.

Having ruled out surrender as the solution to my self-righteous agitation, I decided to at least make hate a nice cup of tea. I sat with it and listened to it. I saw that I was not in charge of correcting it. But to my credit, I didn't run. I was raised to believe that politeness covered a multitude of sins, so I sat there pleasantly, got it a little more tea, then eventually handed it its hat and thanked it for coming. Then I got on with the work I can actually accomplish: Picking up litter. Sending donations to organizations that make the world more fair and kind. (I'll never give up on this.) I am in charge of feeding my animals, as they have no opposable thumbs. I am in charge of making my grandson's lunches. I am not in charge of making legal decisions about gun rights, although I am positive my thoughts about gun rights are the right thoughts, that they are God's thoughts.

I know that if I saw a child hurt an animal, God would agree with me that it wouldn't be a good idea to buy that child a gun when he becomes a teenager. While my tea with hate helped me see my rage toward rabid gun lobbyists, it also allowed me to notice love and compassion for that screwed-up little child who must have been so violated to want to hurt animals. He must have been nearly destroyed, and thus he destroys. (Remind you of anyone?) But I am also sure there are precious, indissolubly good parts in him. The right teacher could work miracles. I was snatched off the path of self-loathing by teachers who were on the ball and saw ways to redirect my fear into creation. This would be my prayer for the child—one amazing teacher.

Ah, prayer. In all the excitement, I'd sort of forgotten to pray. Make me a channel of Thy peace, that where there is hatred, let me sow love, or at least not fertilize the hate with my dainty bullshit.

There was progress over the course of the time I spent in my private hate workshop. There were setbacks, too. The white supremacist rally in Charlottesville, our government's halfhearted response to the hurricane that devastated Puerto Rico. I returned again and again to my favorite hate story in the New Testament, the story of the Good Samaritan, which Jesus tells in Luke. This story would have horrified any good Jew within earshot, as Jews despised Samaritans (long story, family feud). "Good Samaritan" to them would have been a paradox, like "saintly Muslim" to some of our elected officials. They likely would have said, "The only good Samaritan is a dead Samaritan." And yet Jesus makes a Samaritan the hero of the story, because he alone is moved to compassion to help someone in need.

The part I like most about Luke's story is the lawyer who tries to trap Jesus with a trick question about who his neighbor is, so he can find a loophole in Jesus' appeal to love thy neighbor. The lawyer wants to narrowly define *neighbor* so he can say, "In my view, this person is not a neighbor, so I can continue to hate, to fear him and treat him as badly as I want," which is straight from today's front pages. That, I am sorry to admit, is what I might have tried.

Curiously, the word for *moved* is from the word for *guts*: in Jesus' day, Jews thought, somewhat like us, that the strongest feelings resided not in the heart, but in the deepest innards, which are hard—for good reason—to ignore. It is a word that's used elsewhere in the New Testament for what Jesus feels when he looks at ordinary struggling people who don't know how to get through the day. He is *moved*. Can the traveler left for dead be in a position to feel moved, or feel anything other than surprised gratitude for the Samaritan? Is surprised gratitude the same as love? I don't know. But I think it can be where love begins.

Becoming intimate with hate slowly increased my self-respect. I did not inherit the genetic coding to feel sure of myself. (I'm sure your DNA is just *fine*.) Hate helped me meet my inner traffic cop, employed to stand in for self-care, who ticketed and shamed my brothers and me as a misguided public service when we fell short. An innocent mistake.

But there are ways to shake him: surrender, empathy, and celebration throw him off.

To surrender is to give up to. You can hold up your hands, palms forward, like someone is pointing a gun at you, or palms up, begging for help, or arms and hands upward, as if lifting something to the sky. In every case, though, you first have to put down your weapons.

Empathy begins when we realize how much alike we all are. My focus on hate made me notice I'm too much like certain politicians. The main politician I'm thinking of and I are always right. I, too, can be a blowhard, a hoarder, needing constant approval and acknowledgment, needing to feel powerful. This politician had an abusive father, but he managed to stay alive, unlike his brother. I don't think he meant to grow up to be a racist who debased women. But he was raised afraid and came to believe that all he needed was a perfect woman, a lot of money, and maybe a few more atomic weapons. He must be the loneliest, emptiest man on earth, while I am part of a great We, motley old us. We show up, as in the folktale about stone soup, and we bring and give and put what we can into the pot, and this pot fills up, and we know it.

Celebration as a command? How great is that? Outdoor concerts, community hikes, birthday parties, worship services, street fairs. Have another bialy. That's an order.

This country has felt more stunned and doomed than at any time since the assassinations of the 1960s and the Vietnam War, and while a sense of foreboding may be appropriate, the hate is not. At some point, the hate becomes an elective. I was becoming insane, letting politicians get me whipped up into visions of revenge, perp walks, jail. And this was satisfying for a time. But it didn't work as a drug, neither calming nor animating me. There is no beauty or safety in hatred. As a long-term strategy, based on craziness, it's doomed.

No one can take this hatred off me. I have to surrender it every time I become aware of it. This will not go well, I know. But I don't want my life's ending to be that I was toxic and self-righteous, and I don't know if my last day here will be next Thursday or in twenty years. Whenever that day comes, I want to be living, insofar as possible, in the Wendell Berry words "Be joyful though you have considered all the facts," and I want to have had dessert. Maybe insanity will not change to wisdom and a focus on the common good anytime soon, but I can bring less hate to the pot of stone soup, the common well, less of my unbaked cake batter. More rosemary, more carrots. (That is not a bad mantra.)

Hating the way I was feeling helped me give up Camel cigarettes thirty-two years ago, and then alcohol. It is good to surrender things that poison us and our world. Am I free of such toxicity now? Well, about forty percent, and that is a pretty good deal. I'll take it.

Hate weighed me down and muddled my thinking. It isolated me and caused my shoulders to hunch, the opposite of sticking together and lifting our hands and eyes to the sky. The hunch changes our posture, because our shoulders slump, and it changes our vision, as we scowl and paw the ground. So as a radical act we give up the hate and the hunch the best we can. We square our shoulders and lift our gaze.

SIX

Writing

S o, writing. What a bitch. I suppose being any kind of artist is hard at times, most times, and while my aim is to bring hope to anyone creating art, my specialty is writing, so I will use this one modality as shorthand to discuss the challenges of creation.

Writing almost always goes badly for everyone, except for Joyce Carol Oates.

If you do finish what you're writing, you will probably not sell your book, although you may, for much less than you were hoping (or deserve).

No one cares if you continue to write, so

you'd better care, because otherwise you are doomed.

If you do stick with writing, you will get better and better, and you can start to learn the important lessons: who you really are, and how all of us can live in the face of death, and how important it is to pay much better attention to life, moment by moment, which is why you are here.

Sometimes I tell rooms full of adults everything I know about writing, which takes about an hour. Sometimes I tell small rooms full of my young grandson's colleagues a shorter version of the same thing, which takes twenty minutes. The longer version begins with this:

The stories we have loved, beginning with our earliest days, are how we have survived, grown, and not ended up in gutters barking at ants (knock wood). These stories have saved us, like Jesus and the Buddha and Martin Luther King have saved our lives and souls, and Molly Ivins, Mary Oliver, Gandhi, and E. B. White have saved our sanity, our hearts, and our families.

Both versions almost immediately mention that the authors of all the books we love (these salvation stories) knew that the great secret of writing is to keep one's butt in the chair. (My first-graders go crazy at the word *butt*; they could die laughing. Now I've got them where I want them—paying attention is ninety percent of writing.) These authors tell the stories that come through them, one day at a time. I tell the kids an old story: Fifty-five years ago, when my older brother's fourth-grade term paper on birds was due the next day and he hadn't started, my dad sat him down with his Audubon books, paper, and pencils. My brother was in tears. Dad said to him, "Just take it bird by bird, buddy." All he had to do was read and then write about pelicans in his own words. Then chickadees. Then dark-eyed juncos. My brother drew beautifully. Bird by bird, magical things come to be.

My kids know that they get to ask people to read their stories and help make them better, while my grown-up students have forgotten this, how much help we need, deserve, and can ask for. My grown-ups know that if you are a writer, everything that happens is grist for the writing mill, for transformation, and just as important,

Anne Lamott

for revenge. Also, you will have great stories and details to heap into your subconscious mind's buckboard, for later literary use or blackmail.

The first year I gave my grandson's class the writing talk, when he was in kindergarten, the kids paid attention fairly well for five-year-olds. I talked about bird by bird, and writing really poopy first drafts, which they loved. But Jax came up afterward, pulled me aside, and said sotto voce, "Nana, that was terrible."

I was shocked. "What?"

"You said you could teach us how to write books, but you only taught us how to write one bad page." He was disappointed in me, and maybe bitter.

"Oh, dearest," I said. "That's pretty much all I have to offer."

But one bad page a day becomes a book. The only problem is, from where does that page spring?

Memory, research, early-morning visions, and imagination. I tell little kids mostly about the last one, that there is a movie screen in their minds called the imagination, which they can see if they close their eyes. Writing means you scribble down what you can see on the screen and all around you. Close your eyes, or open them and look around, at one another's faces, look out the window at that shameless diva, nature. Wild, right?

I want to tell them to savor and delight in everything they write from now until junior high, because after sixth grade they will never think they are any good at anything. It's never, ever, ever good enough until you learn it's good enough. You need to reestablish the purpose of writing. If it's fame, money, or power, you're doomed. One friend, the loveliest, dearest man you can imagine, thirty years clean and sober, happily married, won an Oscar for a song he wrote—among the greatest achievements for a songwriter. And it bought him one day. One day of self-esteem and satisfaction.

If it's creative release, or you have a story to tell, or if you've just always wanted to write a novel, or you just love to write, the way other people like to garden, you're good.

I once shared this belief at a writing

conference in a place of extraordinary beauty and wealth, in the hourlong version of the talk I give to younger kids. When I got to the part where I promise, swearing on my soul, that publication will not make the writer whole, healed, and joyful, for any length of time, there was an outburst from a seat halfway down the lecture hall. A round, beet-red man about my age, drunk at ten-thirty in the morning, shouted about how wrong I was to say people would not be made whole if they got a book published. Yes, they would! He had made a fortune and was so happy, he yelled, shaking his fist at me, and had been ever since publication. He owned two houses in this town of Alpine beauty. "You are telling these people lies!"

This is not an isolated example. Many of the saddest, meanest, most jealous and destructive people I have known or dated have been highly successful writers. So don't write thinking that publication will fill in the Swiss-cheesy holes in your soul or hoping that it will bring you personal improvement, because it won't. Write because you have to, because the process brings great satisfaction. Write because you have a story to tell, not because you think publishing will make you the person you always wanted to be. There is approximately zero chance of that happening.

When my grandson was in first grade, I asked one of his colleagues to explain to the rest of the class what a story was: "The telling part." That's exactly right. I asked the class if there was another way to say that, but my using the word *say* gave them an unfair advantage, because another child said, "The saying thing, of what happens." Flannery O'Connor once gave her neighbor at the end of the road some of her stories, and when the neighbor returned them, she said, "Well, them stories just gone and shown you how some folks would do."

That is all you need to know—say it, say what happened that seemed worth the telling, or that you don't want to forget. Stories are when something happened that you didn't expect, that lead to some deep internal change in yourself or the main character. Tell it.

Something happened, both to and inside a person, that we need you to help us see, and if you believe it wasn't old and boring, I want to hear it.

And everything that has happened to you belongs to you. If people wanted you to write more warmly about them, they should have behaved better.

I have three good friends who have each been working on their novels for more than five years, and in two of these cases a great deal longer. Every so often, they each share their novel with a friend, an agent, or a random wife, and every time the person tells them the novel is not done yet, which means not yet publishable, which they hear as meaning not that there are some structural problems, but that they are losers, asshats, dilettantes. But then they get back to work, deeply alone with their bad minds, for hours, in their little hovels, completely absorbed, in slightly cranky ways. Why would they do this?

Because it gives them joy. They got to be writers when they grew up, their lifelong dream. Their stories, their memories, imaginations, and images are like treasures in their hearts, springing forth from the ground of being, the common well, things that they alone can tell, in their own voices and language, even if inadequately, with a sense of accomplishment, struggle, concentration, fulfillment, and for a few minutes every few days, pride.

My friends' novels are taking years, because they have to dig deep, and insist on being true to the story, to the story they are called, assigned, or moved to tell, and on being honest about what they found, instead of telling the story they thought or wished they'd found. Writing that carries truth uplifts us, teaches empathy, purpose, dignity. This means taking out the lies and boring parts, and especially the grandstanding sections, which are probably the parts you love most. Jessica Mitford often quoted Arthur Quiller-Couch that you must kill your little darlings. Leave in the nuggets of life, illuminating and compact, where the reader can taste a soupçon of truth, or laugh and have to turn the page, like a child. Three things abideth: voice, a story, a trustworthy narrator; but the greatest of these is story.

The story has to have really happened, even if the writer has made it up. The reader has to trust the truth in a story. We're doing this all the time inside us, reporting to ourselves on what we see, trying to make sense of this life. The stories we tell ourselves and write can warp us or raise us, save or destroy us, illuminate or dissemble.

The stories that younger kids love involve underdogs, like Harry Potter and themselves, who are ridiculed, stuck, trapped, in danger, and yet who find a way out, escape or redemption. These are my favorite stories, too, involving a shift in the point of view, from feeling so doomed, in such a deep hole, without any strength—until this unexpected event happens. We were going from A to B, from one place to another, and then something *changed*. It means there is the possibility of change, in this dark and unfair world, and in us: in this story, I rose up, and now I feel very different. Look at all that was in my way, look what helped, look at this funny detail. The details we choose are what make a story resonate, and when a story resonates, the dust of confusion clears for a few minutes, and things hold together—and how often does this happen in the rest of life?

I tell the kids I teach that a writer is saying:

Take a walk with me. Let's see where this path leads. Two of them get up to leave. No, I say, on paper. They moan with disappointment.

A story begins somewhere in space and time, when you step onto the path beside the writer. Where could that be? Mars, one girl says. Hogwarts, Hawaii, and my favorite, Nicasio, three towns away, population ninety-six. But oh, what some of those people gone and done.

We get to know some characters who are recognizable as family, friends, ourselves, even in their distressing guise as vampires, orphans, or ministers. Events transpire, possibly not all leading to ecstasy or serenity, and people are changed. The universe is usually telling us the same story, that our lives are rich and fluid and infinitely mysterious; that we only thought we were stuck, that nothing stays the same for long.

I tell the kids: Stories are flashlights. You shine a light in one place—an attic floor, a canyon wall, or a memory—and then you describe it the best you can. Maybe you need to find a photo of it in a book, or maybe it is right there in your memory, on the screen behind your eyes.

What a writer is telling us, asking us to hear, has to have meaning. There is really no reason for you to keep shoehorning in cute, charming dinner table anecdotes. Tell us something that stirs us, that makes us think, or tear up, or laugh.

How? You just start talking about it on paper, as you would to a very good friend.

And once you've spewed it out, you can see the details and moments that made you catch your breath and be so glad you remembered this detail and got to share it.

We have to cultivate the habits of curiosity and paying attention, which are essential to living rich lives and writing. You raise your eyes out of the pit, which is so miserable and stifling to be in and which tried to grab you and keep you there, until something sneaky hauled you out and changed you.

I tell my kids to begin by scribbling away, to write one sentence at a time as fast as they can. A writer friend told me, first you spew on paper, then you chew, and then you choose the details that flesh out your story. The characters in your story are real people to you, and include you, but they aren't yet real people to your audience: they weren't there. The specific details are what make it universal, what make it sing. Life is made up of these mosaic moments, seemingly meaningless details that tug on your sleeve to get your attention. My writer friend also said that after you've chewed over your story, you find the frozen moment when the person turns, veers, or was grabbed.

This has to leave you letting out your breath or gasping for it: This is what I saw! It was a trip and important to me, and now this is where I leave you.

Let the energy of your story be the drama— what you've experienced that was so amazing or touching—instead of draping it with Christmas tree lights or sparklers. If we readers sense that you're manipulating us—making the story hot, because you don't have confidence in it—the story loses its beauty, and we turn on you.

A story does not need to be hot. Stories are usually about a modest salvation. Events took us on a journey that was inconvenient or scary, and changed us, in ways that helped us feel more connected to life, made it more spacious and welcoming.

There is a lot about writing that will not make sense for a while to the young kids I teach. Writers save the world—or at any rate, they saved me and everyone I'm close to. When we were small, they were our travel guides and companions in the great mysteries of life and family. They were mirrors, mentors, guide dogs. They helped me laugh about terrifying and isolating things, and made me question my very reason for existence, as well as my fears, prejudices, and illusions. They helped free me from hubris, and thus tunnel vision. They helped heal my pain, in giving me people I recognized, humans as screwed up and narcissistic and dear as I was, whom I was able to respect and enjoy, who had scary and/or profound experiences and discovered courage and grace that maybe I could find, too.

It's ridiculous how hard life is. Denial and avoidance are unsuccessful strategies, but truth and awareness mend. Writing, creation, and stories are food.

But do not tell your family this. They'll want to know if you have an agent.

I tell the six-year-olds that if they want to have great lives, they need to read a lot or listen to the written word. If they rely only on their own thinking, they will not notice the power that is all around them, the force-be-with-you kind of power. Reading and writing help us take the blinders off so we can look around and say "Wow," so we can look at life and our lives with care, and curiosity, and attention to detail, which are what will make us happy and less afraid.

At this point the kids are hanging on my every word, not, as it turns out, because they are thrilled by my talk, but because one little boy has now spread the rumor that I own the local library.

Writing breaks the trance of our belief that the world is going to hell in a handbasket, and we need to protect ourselves and our families at all times. Stories goose us in a good way. The right story can show us how to lighten up. If we tread lightly, hold life lightly, we can look around more bravely. Without blinders on, we are not forced to get life to conform to our convictions, our past pain, or our superior belief system. It turns out there is not just this—there is also that, over there.

For example, at a memorial service, there is deep grief in the room, but also gratitude, love, emptiness, and many kinds of food. At a holiday party, people are decked out in their finery, beaming with cheer, but maybe not doing so fine on the inside. We are this, and not this; that, and not that.

There is so much I want to share with these kids, so they will be readers and writers, storytellers, listeners, and seekers, but we have almost run out of time, and some of this will have to wait for the next class, let alone next year. Then I will tell them that writing will help them see life more accurately. People are little truth-seeking missiles, but not many of us were encouraged to challenge our convictions and identities, except by writers and certain teachers, so we extracted meaning by selecting certain variables that agreed with our parents' worldview. Yet the more variables we decide to include, the greater breadth of writing, the bigger bandwidth of truth, the more our understanding aligns with what truly is;

paradoxically, the more expansively we can see, the more simple truth seems. Imagine the Google eye pulling back from the chaos and clutter of your garage, the jumble of the town where you live, and revealing patterns in the woods, the countryside, the canals and foothills, the crowds gathered to protest or sing.

In later writing workshops, as my grandson grows, I will tell him and his colleagues that it is all so much bigger and wilder than we think, and we can deepen our ability to experience our attention to detail, the pattern on the butterfly's wing, your grandma's wondering eye, how the deep jagged cut on your finger has healed so perfectly. We start to get a hint of the power and sweetness and absurdity of life and to see it not as all fragile or harsh, but as real, the really real. We get buoyancy and, God knows, sometimes even effervescence. Perspective doesn't reduce the gravitas; it increases reverence.

I will tell my fifth-graders that the main reason to be a writer is that it is the perfect antidote to materialism, which drains our soul and spirit. Writing dilutes our habitual fear and our need for control. When they are older, the kids get to decide how to spend their lives: in tightly controlled, hyperachieving ways, putting away childish things, if they so choose. Or they can write.

I tell the first-graders that the truth of the story is in the very telling of it, that if they write me a made-up story, that makes it true. Write me a story right now, I tell these kids. Start where you are, let yourself scribble and write badly. Then make it better. Their teacher and I will help them make it really good later. For now, we are all collectively going to keep our butts in our chairs for a while, okay? They nod. I put my hands on my hips just like my grandson does. "Deal?" I ask sternly.

"Deal," they reply.

Grip those pencils, I tell them, close your eyes, let your heads drop to your chests while you study what is on the screen behind your eyes.

They demonstrate good grippage, close their eyes, and bend their heads as if in prayer to see what is inside.

SEVEN

Bitter Truth

Chocolate with 81% cacao is not actually a food. Its best use is as bait in snake traps. Also, as a shim to balance the legs of wobbly chairs. It was never meant to be considered an edible.

Don't let others make you feel unsophisticated if you reach middle age preferring Hershey's Kisses. So many of your better people do. Also, always carry a handful of Kisses in your backpack or purse to give away. People will like you more.

EIGHT

In the Garden

An elderly friend asked me one day when we wandered through a church garden and it started to rain what three things I would share with her young relative who fears death, as she knows I view death mostly as a significant change of address.

The first thing I told her is that I have been on hand to help people cross over, been there for days and months at the end of a person's life, and while I would prefer that all deaths be swift and sweet, without dementia or pain, every death has been rather beautiful.

Second, the more time you spend in the presence of death, the less you fear it. Your life will be greatly enhanced by spending time with dying people, even though you've been taught to avoid doing so.

Third, death is not the enemy; snakes are. And cheese: it is addictive and irresistible. I have had three kinds so far today.

Shakespeare said we all owe God a death. That's very nice. If I were God's West Coast representative, I would try to work out some of the loan details of having to die. We can all agree that children should be exempt, that dementia should always be the spaced-out dithery kind (and not involve screaming), that pain should always be manageable, and that wars should be avoided through wise diplomacy, goodwill, and political sanity. In lieu of these codicils, though, while people in dreadful pain of any kind may long for the solace of a divine continuing manifestation, what we can offer is to stay with them faithfully. This may not seem like a lot until we show up for you, which we will.

I asked my friend in the garden if I could add

a few more thoughts that might help put her dear relative's mind at ease. This is what I told her.

Anytime you investigate how scary and bad loss is, it becomes a lot less bad, and a lot less bad is a small miracle. The great paradox is that drawing nearer to death will help begin to put it in the rearview mirror. Then, instead of living in unconscious fear of its arrival, crashing our party, we accept it as one of the musicians, like the old donkey on his way to Bremen to play the lute.

And I promise that the people you lose here on this side of eternity, whom you can no longer call or text, will live fully again both in your heart and in the world. They will make you smile and talk out loud at the most inappropriate times. Of course, their absence will cause lifelong pangs of homesickness, but grief, friends, time, and tears will heal you to some extent. Tears will bathe, baptize, and hydrate you and the seeds beneath the surface of the ground on which you walk. Somehow, as we get older, death becomes as sacred as birth, and while we don't exactly welcome it, death becomes a friend.

Death is not whatever you feared as a child.

It's both more interesting and more casual, with fewer worms involved. It is usually doable, astonishing but plain, like notes played without sharps or flats, a natural G instead of A-flat, or succulents instead of roses.

My friend dragged me to look at one corner of the church garden where she had seen an eruption of baby pink tea roses the week before, in similar weather, gray and wet. She said they made up for a lot, including that morning's new threat of nuclear war with North Korea. But when we found them, they had already turned brown.

"I rest my case," I said.

My friend next wanted to show me something else, in a part of the garden where most of the flowers were dormant, so I took her there. At eighty, she knows you don't put things off. And we were charmed.

They were plants called Hens and Chicks, a big succulent with smaller ones clustered beneath and around. They look like a cross between artichokes and lotus flowers, sea-glass green, the newer petals of each mother trimmed in light, the slightly older ones trimmed in rose, with thorns.

I spend a lot of time with old people who know things but maybe need a hand. More than any other sentence I have ever come across, I love Ram Dass's line that when all is said and done, we are all just walking each other home.

The tough little centers of the Hens, where the new petals spring from, looked like children's belly buttons; there were drops of water collected in the centers like diamonds. This was surrounded by a controlled explosion of green joy, all of it expansive and enclosed at the same time—like us.

I always used to be ambivalent about cacti. Pink tea roses were my favorite flower when I was young, because they were pretty and girly, smelling like flowers and tea, the opposite of death. There was no death in the fifties when I was coming up, except for pets. There were just pencil-shaped erasers with bristles at the end, so every last vestige of a person's absence could be whisked away. Death was shooed out of sight, so of course we all grew up terrified. The stories and songs we children whispered to each other involved mostly ghouls, zombies, worms, long bony fingers.

My parents had apparently not read the letter where Rilke wrote: "I am not saying that we should love death, but rather that we should love life so generously, without picking and choosing, that we automatically include it (life's other half) in our love. This is what actually happens in the great expansiveness of love, which cannot be stopped or constricted. It is only because we exclude it that death becomes more and more foreign to us and, ultimately, our enemy." My erudite parents were above being bothered by death. It was something the nutty Catholics down the street seemed concerned with.

The only death and dead bodies we tended to were our darling pets, and the little corpses that they had killed and brought to us. Death meant something was instantly not alive, no longer with you. You saw this most vividly when your pet died. All that unmitigated wriggly love was gone, was so dead, and it was the end of the world.

You saw dead mice and squirrels—once so Beatrix Potter, now reduced to looking like stiff little rugs, miniature bearskins with arched claws.

My parents were not crazy to fear death. It is an instinct to stay alive. My father had fought on Okinawa, my mother had grown up poor in Liverpool—so yeah, stay alive and prosper. Burnish that surface. We don't need any more cold reality.

When you are young, death is so creepy, addressed only in the dark by your friends, who explain to you why you are going to rot in hell for all eternity or spin through outer space forever. (I was told both things. Curiously, I became a lifelong insomniac.) This rang so true.

All children know exactly why they should be punished and thrown away.

My maternal grandmother weighed about seventy pounds when she came to stay with us, when I was six. She had Alzheimer's, which her two daughters, my mom and my cherished aunt, would both die of, too. The person, Nanny, whom I had been used to, was completely vacant—a stranger with a bad attitude. It was as if she had stepped into a chute of total self-absorption, where she didn't care about adorable me. And my paternal grandfather, who had heart disease, couldn't even be visited near the end, and just got vaporized one day.

I was terrified of death, and yet I remember thinking I was immortal. Most kids do. They couldn't be kids if they didn't. They are the green fuse, the energy of growth, the cord stretching from this side to the other, and it is inconceivable that someone, even one of them, might be ripped from the root. Six months before he died, my father said, "I simply cannot imagine a world without Ken Lamott in it." He was fifty-five. Then a long cognitive deterioration, but pain-free, thanks to early hospice. Then poof. Gone.

He was so gone. Dead people look universal— the gaping mouth and locked jaw. Where was the angelic expression of sweet release? The flesh had fallen away, all that life and brilliance transformed into a beaky, craggy face. We closed his eyes and mouth, and then there was something sleepy and peaceful in his face, yet there was also a grotesque finality.

At some point you experience that a body is just the shell of a person, a cocoon that's been outgrown. Hospice showed us how to wash his body; twelve years later, my best friend's body; and each friend after that. This is the sacrament, because our people are still so precious, and when you learn this, you experience it as privilege.

Dearest, if you could just gently tend to the body of a dead person, wash them with a warm soapy cloth, rub oil into their skin, dress them in their favorite clothes—don't forget socks!—and see the love and honor in this, it would greatly diminish your fears.

But until then, fear thrums from deep within, and it is pretty damn scary—the great unknown of absence, the fear that the whole world could be gone in the death of one person, as if a nuclear bomb has fallen. Draw nearer. Do it afraid.

In the church garden, beside the Hens and Chicks, my now favorite plant, I asked my friend if her deceased son still felt present to her, years after he had passed away. She said his energy was still alive and palpable, like her husband's, but not in a way she'd sensed anywhere else. His atoms and his vigor and humor are still around in the ether. When she comes across something that would have pleased her son and husband when they were alive, mostly music or an old vaudeville routine they loved, she can feel the two of them grok it in some peculiar way. The love and energy remained, those fields of atoms that aren't wafted away at death from our familiar sphere.

I have felt this so often, how we flash on our loved ones who've died, which means they are alive in us.

The flash is seeing their face, hearing their voice as clearly as we heard them in this life, teasing and noodling us—"Hey, Annie, aren't you going to pick that penny up?"

They visit—ectoplasmically—and you invite them to come closer, so you are together with them, no longer in separation, together like the individual hen with her brood of chicks. There is a cupping, like a hand, a palm ready to receive and already holding.

When you're younger, especially in your thirties and forties, when you may have stopped taking drugs and drinking quite so much and maybe have had children, all of which destroyed any sense of complacency you may have had, you've seen some deaths, experienced some grave and impossible loss. Maybe you search for understanding, but find only one thing for sure, which is that truth comes in small moments and visions, not galaxies and canyons; not the crash of ocean waves and cymbals. Most traditions teach that truth is in these small holy moments. Even our friend Jesus, whom we don't see acting ebullient very often, expresses pleasure in Matthew 11: "Thank you, Father, because you reveal things to the small and simple and hide them from the clever." (I think he was looking at his disciples then, and fully acknowledged what a sorry bunch they were, and we are, and yet in their way they were *getting* it. They were seeing the glory around for those who have eyes to see, the kingdom within.) "Watch," Jesus says, again and again.

Watch. See the divine presence everywhere,

from the most glorious bearded Tibetan iris, to weeds and grasses, to cacti. Cacti are really amazing once you get to know them. They are much friendlier than they look. They adapt and survive, even though they often live in snake-infested regions, where it is so arid (and scary). They are very resourceful. They seem to have a good time, with small careful moments of de-light, in the live theater of soil, in their fingers and toes.

Because there was that light rain at the church, my friend and I took one last look at a Hen before leaving. There was the thin piping of light around all the petals, the outline that grew rose-colored in the older petals, warmer but not as exciting; fading. We fade, too. It's poignant to see kin and friends who were once so vital grow aged. There is grief at the memorial service, but also gratitude for what the person brought to our lives, amazement at the details in the obituary—who knew about all the places she traveled to, all the volunteering she did? And gratitude is a very bright light. Not the Christian kind, which tends to be transactional—Thank you for this result, or the check; thank you for my gift, or my health; and please don't let anyone take it. Gratitude is seeing how someone changed your heart and quality of life, helped you become the good parts of the person you are. Never will a gathering of people feel a deeper awareness of the present, a longing for immersion in the right now, and to share their love out loud with those they love most, than at a memorial service. This often lasts the whole day.

Of course when certain people die, there is anguish. We will never get over their deaths, and we're not supposed to. A year after my best friend died, another girlfriend asked me, if I could have anything I wanted in the world, what would it be? She said her wish would be that she and her wife stay together forever. I said my wish was to see Pammy one more time. I had a beloved child and a life I enjoyed, but that was what I longed for. Do you think that is crazy?

Later, when time, grief, therapy, and love helped me make a kind of peace, the anguish and obsession became a wistful, nostalgic gratitude. It's not ideal. Yet along with my dad's death and my son's birth, nothing has given me so many gifts of growth, expansion, and knowing myself, which is not always lovely, but it's why I am here.

Most of my spiritual breakthroughs have been against my will. I am mortal, impermanent, imperfect, scared, often uptight and even petty, but wow, what a beautiful sunset. Yes, the Buddha was right about sickness, old age, and death, but check out that moth, that plum. I have not had a near-death experience, but I am having a near old-age one: failing memory, vision, stamina, skin tone. (When my grandson asked, "Can I take a shower with you if I promise not to laugh?" I thought, "You and me both.") Both my parents died too young of advanced brain disease, of brain cancer and Alzheimer's, so I sometimes get a little worried about my condition. Losing the ability to walk made their worlds smaller and smaller, to the size of a bed. The only worlds smaller were their urns.

And for people who manage to live longer than my parents, so many of their friends will have died. There are fewer and fewer people to relate to. To have survived can be lonely. But I

have seen great blessings in the losses of my old-
est friends and church family. Simplification, for
example. Life is richer when it is simple. A walk,
buttered toast, a child's soccer game. You're af-
forded the opportunity to stop doing and can instead just be here. Wow. Yet you don't have to be
near death or have the depth of Thomas Merton
to love and seek it. It's not navel gazing. Contem-
plation is the opposite. It's being a human being,
implicit in the job description, what my very old
friends have loved most at the end. They can't
look anymore to power, stature, schedules, or
fame to fill them up, and they sure as hell don't
feel like entertaining you. All those things turn
out not to have been real and eternal. Love did
and is, that's all.

The reason to draw close to death when we're
younger is to practice finding and living in the
soul. This grows our muscles for living. In the
absence of the illusion of power and majesty, we
see that the soul was right here all along, everywhere, and consequently we can once again feel
charmed by the world.

Can you even imagine living this way,

charmed by the world, in the light of gratitude, for what is real, for the truth of who we always have been and will continue to be, no matter how much ground we lose? I don't think my parents remembered to teach me this. This truly is what it means to be born again.

Thank God my parents exaggerated the danger of death when I was young. It kept me alive, kept me from drowning and getting run over. But now, if I am not careful, this fear keeps me small, cringing. It gets me to check my messages at waterfalls and baseball games. Facing it down got me to visit India. Facing it down let me fall in love at sixty-two. Sixty-two!

When I am sitting next to people who are in the process of transition, I always tell them: Stay as long as you want, and fly away whenever you're ready. Sometimes I read these people poetry or Scripture, but more often I sit with them in silence. I turn off my phone. It is okay to do that, just as it is okay to stare out the window. Maybe it is not spectacular outside, no sunrise or storm clouds, but maybe the sky has the thin bright light of mid-autumn, is a pretty pale blue with small puffs of white clouds above the ridge of the grassy hilltop. Silence is medicine. You may feel overwhelmed with the profundity of the moment, or get really bored, and in either case will want to check your texts. That's okay; many of us do, too. Maybe try not to check so often, though.

Nothing much happens at the bedside. Maybe the person's color changes, maybe their breathing. When petals of the Hen get really old at the base, they sag like droopy bloomers, much redder, rust instead of rose, and they eventually drop to the ground and become part of the mulch. This fills me with hope, their return to the earth, their recirculation. Nothing is wasted. Before we left the garden, my friend and I bent down to touch the papery shroud of a former plant. We grunted and laughed getting up—oof oof. I guess each of the petals has to become part of the soil so they can feed the plant again. The petals go from those tough, muscular baby belly buttons, to big and strong, to fragile, to papery, and then to nourishment—invisible, beneficent, here.

NINE

Hands of Time

Your inside person does not have an age. It is all the ages you have ever been and the age you are at this very moment. As soon as you get used to being some extremely advanced age that you used to think of as ancient and hoary, you will get even older, God willing. Random teeth will fall out of your mouth as you walk to your car. You will rarely feel as old as you are, except when you have just returned from traveling overseas or are in line at the DMV.

I feel and like to think of myself as being forty-seven, but looking over the paperwork, I can see that I was born in 1954. My friend Paul told me in his eighties that he felt like a young man with something wrong with him. If a doctor told me I had some sort of brain or blood disease, my current level of cognition would make sense.

Aging can be hard. It might have been useful had we not followed the skin care rules of the sixties, which were to get as much sun as possible while slathered in baby oil and basking in the glow of a tinfoil tanning reflector. Your inside person, your soul, the innermost baby in the nesting doll of you, is close by when you despair about your neck, your failing vision and drive, but your inside person also knows that with myopia, cluelessness, and tiredness comes grace.

TEN

Jah

The God with whom you are having problems, or whom you hate or ridicule, is not the God we are talking about.

When we talk about goodness, an animating intelligence in the universe and in our hearts or a pervasive positive unity or presence, we are not talking about an old bearded guy in the sky, Parvati, or a Jewish Palestinian baby. We are talking about a higher power, a power that might be called Not Me, a kindness, a patience, a hope, which is everywhere, even in our annoying, self-centered, fraudulent selves.

The lower powers—greed, hatred, addiction,

ignorance—are easy to connect with and describe, but a higher power is not easily defined. It can't be controlled, manipulated, or appropriated. It opens us and heals us and brings us together and turns hearts of stone into human hearts. Anytime you are experiencing love, you are experiencing the God we are talking about. But as novelist David James Duncan says, "God" is the "worst nickname ever."

So what is a good nickname for a positive force greater than ourselves, bigger than we can imagine, way bigger than we are comfortable with, better than we can hope for, deeper than where we can fall, beyond mind and awe, where we can still also believe in geology, evolution, astronomy?

The best name ever is Gitchi Manitou, which means "Great Spirit" in several Native American languages. "Jah" is beautiful because reggae is percussive with hope.

Over the decades, I've suggested many names—Ed, Bubbe, Little Tree. I've already shared most of my God thoughts, as there are only a few:

Not Me. Look up. Be kind. But here's a God story I've never written before, because it is too scary.

I had a friend from San Francisco society who got sober when we were the same age, thirty-two, but I believed in God and she was a proud, lifelong atheist. This didn't ever get in our way of devotion to each other. Kelly was brilliant, hilarious, and had been a really bad drunk, one hundred pounds overweight, living in her car. She had gotten sober in AA, and for the first ten years went to a lot of meetings. She looked and dressed like her old upscale self, which is to say a lot of the plaid that only the very wealthy or Russians can get away with (and I'm not a hundred percent sure about the Russians). She became a prestige realtor, got married, stayed sober.

We lived for movies, our dogs, and each new season of *Survivor*, spending hours on the phone discussing every episode and contestant.

Then over lunch one day, she mentioned two teensy details—that she was getting divorced, and had stopped going to her AA meetings. "The God stuff drives me crazy," she said.

"But don't they let you come up with a higher power of your choice?" I asked. "Like the mountain, say, or the ocean? What about your dog? Dog love is god love."

"Dogs are dogs. Friends are friends. I don't believe in a higher power. It's infantilizing."

My friend Don, who was dying of emphysema and alcoholism at the time, decided to experiment with the idea that a caring force outside himself was with him in his last months. He called this higher power his old HP. Then he began to call it his Old Hewlett-Packard. It was silly and made him smile instead of worry so much. That's a very God thing, and "my old HP" is a great name for God.

I told this to Kelly.

"Nah," she said. "The whole God thing wrecks the valuable parts of the meetings, the support and humor. It turns it all into Vacation Bible School."

"But those meetings helped you stay sober, even with the God biz. What about using Good Orderly Direction?"

She rolled her eyes.

I had one more of my famous good ideas. "Emerson said the happiest person on earth is the one who learns from nature the lesson of worship. This is a good place to begin. Go outside and look up."

I thought she would say, "Nature is nature," but instead, she put up her palm like a traffic cop.

"Stop," she said sternly.

My good ideas for other people so often seem to annoy them.

She lost her house in the divorce. It had been a nest of comfort and creation, and a container, the illusion of protection. It had held her and her beloved dog. They had to move to a more affordable county.

Kelly and I didn't see each other as much after that. We talked on the phone every month or so. After getting fleeced in the divorce, she stayed sober, but she reported that she was steadily regaining the weight she had lost. We met for lunch every few months, and while she was still stylish and game, she had outgrown the plaid wardrobe, the ersatz Chanel suits, and her dog had grown old and sick. She mentioned how terrified she was of dying alone. I did not give her my talk on the immortality of the soul. I listened, nodded, and thought about taking on her dog's vet bills.

Like everyone, I have been in dire, searing straits before, when life has pulled the rug out from under me and all my nice Jesusy beliefs have been shaken, when almost everything I am afraid of—loss, failure, crucial deaths—has appeared. These threats and losses could have thrown me into hopelessness, but the rich love of my friends and my crazy consignment-store faith eventually pulled me back to my feet. I could let my breath out again. You never get over certain losses, but the anguish part eventually ends, and it all just sucks for a while.

There were moments when I understood that there was nothing much I was going to understand or figure out. There was simply the present moment, awareness, impermanence, birdsong, love. There is no fixing this setup here. It seems broken and ruined at times, but it isn't: it's simply the nature of human life.

Kelly had other good friends, too, but they

didn't translate for her into a path of living, the belief that there was a force she could turn to. Friends are friends. So she would turn to me when she got stuck or too sad, and I would give her the same advice God always gives me if I think to ask: Go do some anonymous things for lonely people, give a few bucks to every poor person you see, return phone calls. Get out of yourself and become a person for others, while simultaneously practicing radical self-care: maybe have a bite to eat, check in with the sky twice, buy some cute socks, take a nap.

Then Kelly's dog died. Her world came crashing down. She dropped out of life.

She had nowhere to go, so she stayed inside. I could never figure out why, if she had had such a great initial ten years in AA, she stopped going, but faith-wise and in fact life-wise, "Figure it out" is not a good slogan. To paraphrase Paul Tillich, the opposite of faith is not doubt, but certainty. If I could say one thing to our little Tea Party friends, it would be this: Fundamentalism, in all its forms, is ninety percent of the reason the world is so terrifying. (For the record, three percent is the existence of snakes. Seven percent is general miscellany.) The love of our dogs and cats is the closest most of us will come to knowing the direct love of God on this side of eternity.

Kelly did not have to have a clue about what a higher power was, but she refused to doubt her atheism. She was a fundamentalist. Her great hope was that she could lose weight.

Hope and peace have to include acceptance of a certain impermanence to everything, of the certain obliteration of all we love, beauty and light and huge marred love. There is the wonder of the ethereal, the quantum and at the same time the umbilical. Don't call it God if that lessens it for you. Call it Ed. Call it Shalom. The Quakers, who are not as awful as most other Christians, call it the light.

Kelly and I spoke routinely during each new season of *Survivor*, but we stopped getting together much. I would call sometimes and ask her to lunch, but she wanted to catch up only by phone; she had gained back sixty-five pounds and was renting a room in Oakland from a quiet family. Otherwise, she insisted, she was doing fine.

I think you know where this is headed.

Fifteen years after we both got sober in 1986, she drank again. It started out well enough. As she described it to me from a bed at one of Oakland's public hospitals, she had had two glasses of gin on Tuesday, a pint by Thursday, a fifth on Friday, and then had fallen and split her head open. The mom in the quiet family called 911.

"So much for my best thinking, right?"

I said, "Ay yi yi," finally almost willing to release her to her own destiny, whatever that was. Yet I prayed for her to stay alive until she got the miracle.

This is not where the story ends, but it is what it took her to get back to her meetings, which she attended faithfully for three months. She moved into a studio apartment with a garden. Then the God stuff got to her again, and she stopped going to AA meetings but stayed sober.

"I think there are meetings for atheists," I

mentioned again, with, coincidentally, a printed schedule in my back pocket. Again, she held up her hand in the traffic cop position.

We went back to our *Survivor* postmortems. I decided to respect her free will and not foist my remedial God curriculum on her, my way of helping people who have asked how to begin experiencing God, *asked* being the operative word here. I begin by encouraging people to play, and share, and enjoy. I encourage them to pay attention to their experiences with nature and their connections with others, to anything that gives them direction, a second wind, a bit more energy, a connection. Do I think Kelly having so many years of *Survivor* and me was God in this world? I do. I actually do.

I would never, ever pound any particular text. The Dalai Lama said that "religion is like going out to dinner with friends. Everyone may order something different, but everyone can still sit at the same table." Various Scriptures are the stories of people trying to understand life, its beauty and its impossible hardship, so they tell stories. The overarching story is how we go from tribal gods to the Beloved, the growth and evolution from animal sacrifice to the United Nations. It is the story of noticing power when we pay attention to the sun, or the wind, or the mountain. There's power here that is not a vague and abstract thing. There's power in oil, in water, in silence, and in bread. There is great power in music, which brings us energy and connects us with our own beating hearts, and to others, and reveals the sublime—in the crashing of waves, in drumming, and in the silence between notes. Artists say, "Let me draw something that might help our understanding, help us change or wake up, be inspired to awe or kindness."

I encourage seekers to practice trust. Maybe your family was not as well adjusted as you hoped, and trust does not come easily to you. Is there something I can trust and belong to, or is it just me and my AK-47?

Play is also part of developing trust. Play opens the heart and gives delight and focus, like an abacus did when we were young. Smartphone calculators? Not so much.

Kelly said to me once: "Play is play. Play

doesn't have to be or lead to anything else but fun."

But what about the bigger things it can give you—the open heart, the happy exhaustion, the present moment, something beyond you, which is people to play with? It's the peace of concentration, it's a welcome—"I'm so glad you're here!" Play is learning how to wait, how to applaud someone else's success, how to let others go first. It's reciprocity and laughter. It's very simple and it brings us deeply into the Now, and just for a while, maybe for the rest of the day, you don't have to judge yourself or kill anyone.

I began to be afraid that Kelly would kill herself. I don't have a moral position against suicide. A number of family friends were not able to make it here and they got out. Their life was misery and was getting worse, and they could not help destroying other people's lives. Why stick it out? I believe God is close by however you cross over. But meetings and sobriety had given Kelly a new life once, and maybe they would again.

"Annie, I have got three houses on the

market. I need to get back on my feet. God and meetings are not going to do it."

I once saw a boys' soccer game on YouTube where a Japanese team trounced a team of little American boys. Many of the American boys started to cry. The Japanese team came over and instead of gloating or doing the postgame high-five lineup, they hugged the American boys, exhorting them: "You were so good to play against. Wow! Next year I bet you're going to win."

I just hoped Kelly's friends and I could help keep her alive and sober until something quirky caught her by surprise. But she chose to stay alone. God is often in solitude and quiet, through the still, small voice—in the breeze, not the thunder. But isolation is different from solitude, and Kelly started drinking again.

I hoped her life would turn topsy-turvy enough to get her attention. Topsy-turvy is often a symptom for the presence of God—the last become first, the hungry are fed, the obnoxious are welcomed.

We have to make ourselves available to one

another, or we can't experience goodness. It's not so much us seeking God, tracking Her down with a butterfly net; it's agreeing to be found. The Old Girl reaches out to *everyone* and wants to include us in this beautiful, weird, sometimes anguished life. All people: go figure. These days are among the hardest we will ever live through. The wind is blowing, but because we are together in this, we have hope. Most days. Maybe more than ever before in my lifetime, my friends and I are aware of our brokenness and the deep crazy, the desperation for light, hope, food, and medicine for the poor. What helps is that we are not all crazy and hopeless on the same day. One of us remembers and reminds the rest of us that when it is really dark you can see the stars. We believe grace is stronger than evil and sin. We believe love is stronger than hate, that the divine is bigger than all huge egos simmered together in a bloviation stew, and this makes us laugh. And laughter is hope. We believe and hope that we will get through these terrifying times.

Jesus says we need to approach God and life

like children, not like bossy white alcoholic women with agendas, good ideas, and meeting schedules in their back pockets, so I gave Kelly space. I mailed her Roz Chast cartoons, but it was too painful to see her when she'd been drinking, and our visits dropped off further. We still spoke in the mornings, especially during a *Survivor* season. I simply tried to extend my love and welcome to her without any hope of rescuing her, which is hard for me to grasp with my flinty little Protestant brain.

I called her to the bitter end, dreading it some days. Like the rest of us, I am a mixed grill of beauty and self-centeredness, pettiness and magnanimity, judgment and humility. On a bad day, I'm pushing old ladies on the *Titanic* out of the way to get to the lifeboats. (They're old, they're going to die.) When I pray, I have more good days. I tend to do more service to the poor and lonely, where joy resides. So I'd call her, and listen and love her.

Survivor was the collagen that, no matter how drunk she was getting, held us together. It was the green shoot through which our love flowed. The divine is so eccentric. It is usually regarded as powerful but other times as weak (the baby, the crucifixion), and sometimes it appears absent altogether. Sometimes when I can't see God, I try not to see the divine as more-powerful-than, but just think that it outlasts, like in *Survivor*: loving community will outlast our present darkness and cruelty. Mr. Einstein said that the fourth world war will be fought with sticks and stones. My belief is that even then there will be mercy, goodness, and loving-kindness.

Sometimes I believe that we are here in the world and that God lives upstairs, but other times that we exist on a horizontal axis, running from past to present to future, tracing with a lot more faith than we can usually muster the divine plan of loving community as it unfolds, and (faith tells me) prevails.

When my son first got sober, he had no truck with God except that he was still alive and getting well because of a Group of Drunks. Then he discovered the *National Lampoon* satiric poem

"Deteriorata," in which God may be seen as a hairy thunderer, or a cosmic muffin. For years my son called his higher power The Muffin, as in "The Muffin is showing off today." On messy days, both of us still beseech The Muffin for a hand, a break, a few crumbs of love.

The human condition is both the mess and the tenderness. I don't think love is sovereign in our world in the sense that it can be summoned on cue as if by magic and that once summoned it lingers forever. It's more that if we are lucky, we experience moments of love as a gift between people, and between people and the divine. A whiff may have to be enough sometimes. The universe seems to know we are always alone; we get pushed out at birth, into the cold and the too loud and the too bright, and this provides us with the incentive and the chance to discover connection, warmth, solace—ourselves, in other words.

I tried to stay with Kelly as her pain and craziness increased, but she couldn't bear this. She preferred to be barricaded in the shame and malfunction and booze. I understood that. I asked her to the movies. I asked if I could come over with barbecue. But she could not stand for me to see her at her highest weight in twenty years.

One day she shared good news. "I have a close friend," she assured me, "the older lady upstairs. She's great, brilliant, she's one of us. We eat together most nights, at her place. You'd love her."

"Can I come meet her?"

"One of these days. She's huge, too. She has cancer but she's in remission. I try to help take care of her, and that makes me happy. I visit every day. We absolutely accept each other. We have cocktails, and watch TV, and laugh like crazy."

She told me funny and affectionate stories about the large brilliant woman upstairs the last time we talked. Then she stopped calling me back. She preferred life in the tunnel of her own making, which of course most of us do. You can't force people to be willing to face their pain and anger, to own the ugliness that is in all of us. You can't. I've tried so hard.

The two of them killed themselves together

not long after that, upstairs at the older woman's apartment. They were quite drunk. This broke my heart at first. But later I was glad that Kelly was numb and not alone; that she was with a friend, the loving woman upstairs, which is another good name for God.

I was glad Kelly had a short death. That she was released, that she didn't die a long wet death in the bottle.

What if she had been willing to give up three percent of the identity she was committed to being, the fundamentalist atheist, and entertain the concept that there was something, anything, greater than herself? Anything! Three percent! Who knows if that might have led to another long patch of sobriety? She stayed loyal to her family's isolation and beliefs, barricaded from the world. She had created a fort, like my grandson's fort of sheets and pillows, that is soft and in which you can hide. This is alcoholism. When it tumbles down, some people take your hand. We know what it is like, and we want you to be part of us. You are welcome here. Here, have some of my tea, it's still hot. That is God.

I was so glad Kelly had a friend she let in, one of us, kind and funny, and that I had Kelly for all those years. She was a lovely person, so full of life. Her essence was absolutely still coming through, undamaged, especially in her affectionate stories about her friend upstairs. Essence can never be hurt. It was right there, in her stories. Is this proof of something, that soul and life force cannot be destroyed? I don't know what much of anything means, but I do think so.

Kelly's brothers had a memorial service for her. People cried and roared with laughter, they missed and experienced her in the big funky room where all those sober alcoholics have meetings all day, every day, where she had been welcomed and nursed back to health, given a home. If that isn't God, what is?

I wish good things lasted forever. That would work best for me. But God is a lot more subtle than I am comfortable with. Saint John wrote that God is Love, that anytime you experience kindness and generosity, hope, patience and caring, you are in the presence of God. Anytime you express these, you are drawing something

I would call God into the world. That is how ordinary and accessible God is—meals, TV, visits, laughter, and especially friendship, which made Kelly share with us the things that finally made her feel safe, there in the room upstairs.

ELEVEN

Food

Try to do a little better. Try to be nicer to yourself and to your body. That's all.

Except do not, under any circumstances, start a new diet on Monday, or January 1, or maybe ever again. Diets make us fatter. Why commit to hunger and crankiness if we are almost certainly going to fail and gain back whatever we lose? Is it the secret exhilaration of early weight loss? The sense of control and moral superiority? The dream that our lives and health will more closely resemble TV commercials, the dream that this time we'll keep it off?

You may not mind living this way, but what if

your kids spend their lives chasing these same dreams, embracing the lies and toxic obsession, the secret disgust at their bodies?

I used to start diets, too. I hated to mention this to my then therapist. She would say cheerfully: "Oh, that's great, honey. How much weight are you hoping to gain?"

No one talks to me that way.

I got rid of her sorry ass.

Well, okay, maybe not then. It was ten years later, after she had helped lead me back home to myself, to radical self-care, to friendship with my own heart (and thighs), to a glade that had always existed deep inside me, to (mostly) healthy eating that I'd avoided all those years by achieving, dieting, bingeing, pleasing people, and so on.

She was a tour guide through the battlefield that food had been in childhood. My mom, who was ferociously gifted in the kitchen, was so unhappy in her marriage that she stuffed it all down and became quite heavy. She was short, round, red, and fearless. My father was tall and lean, and in an act of revenge and one-upmanship, he became a great cook, too.

Meals at our house were arctic, served at a beautiful dining table in an igloo.

My mother was always on a diet, except when she was bingeing. When she binged, it was in secret. I learned to diet and to overeat in secret, which is just the best.

Dieting, as with all forms of trying to control our beastly instincts, is about the fear of death. There are people who have overcome this fear, recognizing that making friends with destiny is the way home to freedom, but they are not always the best conversationalists.

It is okay to fear death. Many people who don't can be a little too pleased with themselves. But for our purposes here, let's say that most people overuse things like food, alcohol, drugs, shopping, work, and porn to avoid what they don't want to feel—and mostly what we don't want to feel is fear. If I were God, overconsumption would work better, without such bad consequences, i.e., waking up the next day with a hangover, or a food baby, or divorce papers. By extension, dieting and deprivation and all the jollier aspects of Calvinism should work. But they don't.

Secretly overeating serves the same purpose as dieting: to numb bad feelings, although then, of course, it causes shame and regret. But it is a lot more fun than dieting to sit down in front of the TV with half a carrot cake, or onion dip for ten and a bag of Ruffles. It is unabashed rooting around at the breast, or at the earth like truffle pigs. Shoveling food down is theoretically so comforting; it's a break from the whole world. But because it comes from outside us, it is the same dry fretful breast many of us nursed at. Here, at the mixing bowl of brownie batter or mashed potatoes, is our earth mother in her distressing guise as carbs; as dough.

I learned to hate certain kinds of female bodies, i.e., that of my mother, who was pear-shaped and whom my father found repulsive. I learned to idealize the bodies of the women my father loved, i.e., the taller and long-legged women whom it goes without saying my mother hated. I am both fairly tall and pear-shaped. As you might expect, I learned to hate my body, except during those fabulous years of anorexia, drug use, and personal catastrophe. When my dad and later my best friend were dying, I got down to 112 pounds, which is twenty-five pounds less than now. I loved it so much. (Except of course for the part about my father and my best friend dying. So there was that.)

It took getting older, the greatest friends, years of therapy and unending self-forgiveness to heal the damage I caused myself around food, my body image, and the effects of early old age.

Left to my own devices and without a lot of help, I still believe there are only two major female bodies: us, the pears, all butts and thighs, with grievous cellulite; and the women with long legs, who in middle age get big tummies. They hate their tummies, but we pears hate and resent their long legs and think they don't have any real problems and that they should go the hell away and run around town in their little shorts. (Actually, there are also the naturally thin people, but there are so few naturally thin people that they don't really matter, and no one likes them anyway.)

Two decades ago, the authors of a book called *When Women Stop Hating Their Bodies* posed a question that ruins my life whenever I remember it. I hope it does not ruin yours: What if, no matter what you did or didn't eat, you'd always weigh exactly what you weigh today, never gaining or being able to lose a pound?

The idea filled me with doom—it killed the hope of ever looking twelve again; that the life-long jig was up and now all that was left for me was to have a life with flab and droop. On bad days I wanted to offer the authors a deal: How about we revisit this question in a few weeks, when I could be five pounds lighter? When I asked my partner how he would respond, he said he'd settle for the extra ten he is carrying, if it wouldn't lead to twenty. One friend said she would binge every day for the rest of her life and in fact would do very little else, except maybe also start cutting.

I have experienced hard-fought diminishment of the obsession with food and weight. I swim in warm water in public, in people's pools and at beaches every chance I get, and the shame is way down. But in the weeks before each regal beachly appearance, I always try to lose weight. I don't go for brutal training programs, but I do secretly stop eating carbs, fats, or whatever. Science proves again and again that all diets work briefly, and pretty much all work the same, with initial and exhilarating weight loss, then plateau, then weight gain and shame. The weight we lose almost always finds its way back home, and it invariably brings friends. This, I think, has to do with childhood injuries to our sense of value, with anxiety, and with the inability of our poor parents to nurture consistently, and dieting cannot heal this. Look around at your family and friends, at how many have lost and then regained ten or fifteen pounds just this year. I don't mean to discourage you. Maybe you have a secret-decoder-ring plan not to gain back the weight this time. Yay.

My therapist said starving and dieting are like putting ice cream on a leg wound. I said that ice cream would feel cool and numbing. She said yes and then it would melt.

So what wouldn't melt?

Well, this brings us full circle, to just trying to do a little better, today. That is the secret of life.

Is that discouraging? It is and it isn't. The good part is that you don't have to start blending your coffee with Tibetan yak butter. (That's a lot.) You don't have to pee onto tiny sticks to maintain ketosis and its delightful vomity breath.

Eventually one has to find a way to eat and be kind to one's body. I am not a metaphysician, but this is the body you're going to have the entire time you are here. The only nourishment that can give a body and soul the feelings we crave is profound self-love and union with that scared part of ourselves. Horribly, but as is always the case, only kindness, forgiveness, and love can save us. Oh, and grace, as spiritual WD-40. And walks are nice.

Love means care of, respect for, and delight in our own selves and bodies. The delight part may seem a bit of a stretch, but there's no way around it. "God is love," we Christians like to re-mind ourselves, and every act of love highlights God in the world, because love is not just an idea. Love is something alive, living, personal, and true, the creating and nourishing power within life. It is patient, free to all, and it is medicine and food. This may look like rubbing lotion into your jiggly thighs, patting your stomach as if it is a relative you love: "Why, hello there, Auntie." Love looks like the laying on of hands.

The opposite of love is the bathroom scale.

Putting away the scale is important for all but a few people. If you are one of those people who weigh themselves every day for some healthy reason—other than scaring or shaming yourself, congratulating yourself, or reassuring yourself that you are a good person because you've kept your weight down—then weigh away. Otherwise, can you put the scale away for a week? How about four days? I have been addicted to the scale, too, which is like needing Dick Cheney to determine my value as a human being every morning.

Can you also put away your tight pants, the ones that actually hurt you? Wear forgiving pants! The world is too hard as it is without letting tight pants have an opinion on how you are doing, and make it clear that they are disappointed in you.

At the same time, it feels great to be healthy, and some of you may need to be under a doctor's care. But people like to chirp, "Nothing tastes as good as thin feels," and this is one of those idiocies a certain kind of rage-filled person likes to say, along with "God doesn't give us more than we can handle." I will tell you some things that definitely taste better than thin feels—crème brûlée, lasagna, and all Mexican food except menudo. No one needs to join a gym or live on weight-loss-franchise frozen food, like a tortured astronaut, to be healthy, or eat kale smoothies or hire a bossy trainer. It won't work. You will lose weight quickly, and gain it all back, plus five, minimum. Some of you need to get outside and walk for half an hour a day, or do wheelchair exercises. Mostly, except for my friend Janine and the one percent of the population with celiac disease, you do not have to give up gluten. In fact, I always order extra gluten.

But I have a serious problem with sugar. If I start eating it, I often can't stop and don't want to. I don't have an off switch, any more than I did with alcohol. So sometimes, for weeks or months at a time, I give up sugar. I'm glad when I lose weight, and feel ripped off when I gain it back.

Given a choice, I will eat Raisinets until the cows come home, and then those cows will be tense and bitter, because I will have gotten lipstick on the straps of their feed bags. But we crave what we eat, so if I go for three or four days with very little sugar, the cravings are gone. I love this and it is not dieting. If you are allergic to peanuts, maybe don't eat peanuts.

It's really okay, though, to diet if you need to, for whatever reason, or to binge, and also to have (or pray for) an awakening around your body. It's okay to stop hitting the snooze button and to wake up and pay attention to what makes you feel okay about yourself, one meal at a time. Unfortunately, it's yet another inside job. If you are not okay with yourself at 185 pounds, you may not be okay at 150, or even 135. The self-respect and peace of mind you long for is not in your weight. It's within you. I resent that more than I can say. But it's true. Finding a way to have a relatively safe and healthy relationship with food is hard, and it involves being one's own very dearest person. This will not cause chaos or death, as you were surely taught, but rather an environment where you can drown out the many mean and mistaken voices.

There is the $66 billion American diet industry whispering sweet nothings everywhere you turn. There is your family's jealousy or mortification about your body. There is our own dispirited stance toward ourselves, designed to protect us and advance our potential. There are also the convincing voices of mindfulness, coaching us to eat slowly and to savor taste and texture bite by bite; but to be blunt, this isn't going to happen. While I am not advocating for the school of Shovel and Stuff, to sit chewing so methodically starts to argue a wasted life.

Maybe some of us can try to eat a bit more healthfully, and walk a bit more, or wheelchair dance, and make sure to wear pants that do not hurt our stomachs or our feelings. Drinking more water is the solution to many problems. Doing a three-minute meditation every day may change your life: It is the gateway drug to slowing down. Naps are nice, too.

Almost Everything

Otherwise, without intervention, we may notice each hot new diet. There is no proposal so absurd that thousands of desperate dieters will not buy the book. (My personal recent favorite, right after the caveman and baby food diets, was based on the noble Viking lifestyle, raiding your neighbor's grain stores and salted venison lockers, shopping for foraged vegetables, fatty fish, and moose meat.) The definition of insanity notwithstanding, how many times have you stopped eating carbs, or fats, or processed foods? How did that go?

What gives me hope is how three of the sturdier women at my church got healthier by consciously preparing their meals as if they had asked our pastor or me to lunch or dinner. They wouldn't say, "Here—let's eat standing up in the kitchen. This tube of barbecue Pringles is all for you. I have my own." They wouldn't ask, "Have you gained a little weight? Have you thought about trying the new Viking diet? Yes? Here—have some moose." No, they'd set the table, get out pretty dishes, and arrange delicious foods on the plates. They would cook and serve whole

159

foods, not dish up frozen foods with a dozen in-
gredients, including unpronounceable additives
and petroleum products. There would be grapes
or lemons for color, roasted pumpkin seeds for
crunch. Those plates would be filled with love,
pride, and connection. That care is what we have
longed for our whole lives, and what we create
when we are kinder to our bodies and our hungry souls.

TWELVE

Famblies

If the earth is forgiveness school, family is your postdoctoral fellowship. Family is hard hard hard, a crucible. Think Salem witch trials, or Senator Joseph McCarthy and House Un-American Activities Committee, great pain from which great transformation arises. The family is the crucible in which these strange entities called identities are formed, who we are and aren't but agreed to be. Even in what might pass as a good family, every member is consigned a number of roles intended to keep the boat of the family afloat, which because of the ship's rats— genetics, bad behavior, and mental illness—is

Anne Lamott

not as easy as it sounds. It's the hardest work we do, forgiving our circumstances, our families, and ourselves. Parenting is hard, and so is old age. And every single teenager is hard—even twelve-year-old Jesus drove his folks crazy. (And no word at all on the high school years; like Obama.) Babies are hard. In-laws are hard. And forgiveness is hardest of all.

I was given the role of perfect child at an early age, with disappointment arising from my extreme sensitivity, migraines, and nappy hair. The role of problem child had already been assigned to my older brother. Then I was mommy's big-girl helper and daddy's sweetheart. I was eventually my baby brother's other mother. I was the reliable one, the diplomat, the trusted secret-keeper, the class brain and class clown. And this was all by kindergarten. I grew out of the migraines and grew into my hair, but I am still the world's best big-girl helper, the reliable one, the overly sensitive child, a perfectionist, and so on.

Why give up these identities? Maybe because they gravely limited and falsified my life. And because they aren't who I am. But I like the containment, and how they keep me safe, confined and shipshape, like spandex. When I wear those roles, I can't feel the air on my skin, but by the same token, I'm not exposed.

My favorite role was diplomat, until I called one of my uncles a scumbutt.

I had not asked to be given the role of child statesman, of arranging back-channel negotiations between my parents and siblings whenever called on to do so, like Colin Powell in a red plaid kilt. I didn't know I could turn down the job. I took it on, and I liked it: identity is a posture that we steal and assemble as a protective coating, but it's also a ski mask, camouflage and protection from the cold.

As a girl, I put together a human-appearing persona for the world. We all take on many roles, whether we deserve them or not: good wife, devoted father, dutiful child, do-gooder, rebel, witch. I may be a loser, but I have the belief that I have an upper layer of winner. I may be a winner, but deep down I know I'm a loser, a fraud, a cipher.

The love of family is so central to our lives that if you slip up—say, by calling your uncle a scumbutt, and I might add, in the next breath, a morally bankrupt human being—it throws the carefully crafted mobile into a spinning, tangling mess. But I swear, it was an accident.

This was thirty-some years ago, and there was a modest amount of money involved in the flare-up (I know, what a surprise). My uncle was managing a small collective family fund in a thumb-on-the-scale way. I was representing my brothers' interests and mine, and lately things had gotten clipped and tense. Luckily my brothers and I were still drinking. My older brother called me to say that I needed to call my uncle and explain our position as diplomatically as possible, and after one more cool refreshing beer I set out to do just that. In less than a minute, things went bad.

I listened to my uncle's rationalization for ripping us off, then said this horrible thing and slammed the phone down. It rang almost immediately. It was my older brother, checking back in.

"Hey," he asked, "how did it go?"

Almost Everything

It put a strain on the relationship between my uncle and me for a decade or two. And when I got sober a few years later, it didn't improve immediately, as I had hoped. I prayed for us to have healing, and banked on time, failing memories, and the inevitable arrival of new, fresher family dramas to turn our collective attention to.

I sat out family gatherings for a while. I prayed for my uncle's well-being, for him to have everything I longed for: security, peace of mind, good health, joy. But my uncle was not heavily into the joy business. He was nervous and somehow managed to seem clipped and dithery at the same time. He thought I was a religious nut, which maybe I am. I thought he was missing some essential wiring.

Jesus' message is that who your family says you are has nothing to do with the truth of your spiritual identity. He says that we can all be annoying, petty, misguided, and seem cuckoo to Aunt Muriel and cousin Bob, but that we are in fact perfect children of Light, and that he loves us more than life itself, and that nothing we do can get God to stop adoring us, but He or She would not object to more of an effort toward active goodness and mercy, even when we feel misunderstood and cranky. Jesus says we are made of the same stuff he is, that we are perfect expressions of love, all evidence to the contrary, and somewhere—maybe in Matthew, though don't quote me—he says the most important words of all: "Don't be a big whiny baby." These are both true at once, and again, not what your family told you.

I love my family, my brothers, their wives and kids, my son and his child, my aunts and uncles and my cousins and their kids and spouses. The center of my life has been to try to keep our family together, all of us, even this one man who has never liked me, even before my little episode. I somehow knew that he was a fun-house mirror, No. 2 in birth order, like me, Dutiful Child, which translates as "filled with rage," taught to self-destroy, and to cultivate favor. But he loved me. That's the catch, the rub.

The family package usually comes with food, shelter, and fraught companionship, yet it also includes boredom, fear, and prejudice. It provides a structure that can be tricky to navigate, like a jungle gym. The terrible weight of family is that you may love them, but you also know them too intimately, their dark sides, their secrets and lies. You adore your kids, your nieces and nephews, but you know what they are in for: the world will let them down, hurt them, and try to squelch their spirits so they will be better employees. The world is Lucy teeing up the football. The world is a mean, weepy alcoholic who wants to date your kids. They should have armor, guns, and why—come to think of it, you! Yay, you—bodyguard, banker, nurse.

The good part of false identities is that they kept us alive. They kept us overachieving. The family has to be a cauldron of challenges and loss, or we couldn't grow. But the cost is so high—the held breath, the lifelong fear of being ambushed or unmasked. Do we have time to notice the baby-fingernail moon, a thick cape of morning mist, the diamond dew? Do we play anymore, step away from tasks, duties, and habits with curiosity? Tread carefully: if you are not vigilant, this may lead to wonder, which is joy, which every fear in you knows will lead to job failure and lost revenue.

So often our focus is on supporting the identities and structures that were put in place for us by the more powerful damaged people in the family as caricatures of themselves. Giving up even one of these identities can be threatening to the organism. But the willingness to change comes when the pain of staying where you are is too great, like Anaïs Nin losing her willingness to stay tight in a bud.

After I attacked my uncle, I became willing to look at "diplomat."

Families are hard partly because of expectations, that the people in them are supposed to mesh, and expectations are resentments under construction. You know one another's resentments and dreams better than anyone else ever has, until you each meet your chosen family. Another expectation is that knowing your relatives, and their knowing you so well, should somehow smooth out conflict. Ha ha. We are naked in the family; our worst dangliest bits show. You can't hide much within the cell membrane of a house.

We were raised to believe and expect that blood would be an emollient, but it turned out that we, the children, were the emollients. What linked us all was what didn't work, because that is what got everyone's attention.

It shocks me how hurtful and annoying we can be to the people in our families. We know the soft spots on one another's turtle shells. The weight of family makes us helpless, and in trying to make sure the helplessness doesn't utterly flatten us, we may throw the dart at someone else.

The underdog needs to be hyperattuned to everything going on in order to survive, and everyone in the family is the underdog—except of course, Dad. Dad is Dad, king of the cannibal island, like Pippi Longstocking's father. It had probably always been hard for him to articulate his deep need for love, beauty, and authenticity, so maybe—just guessing here—he was afraid and closed off. Mother, the mom cat, never felt appreciated. She always wanted love, but it was dicey to let her love us because it was all so loaded, with her voracious needs, her thwarted expectations and ambitions. She was scary and

maybe just a bit homicidal. Any mother over-
flowing with love for her tender offspring wishes
at times that the trapdoor would open and swal-
low them up. I was so petty and mean to my
mother when I was a teenager. My older brother
and I disliked each other and never got along:
he was the one in the family who always wanted
to escape, and I was the one who always felt
that someone else was getting the better deal.
We were desperate to be praised, but what was
handed to us by our parents was all the stuff we
didn't do right, or could do better, or had better
be able to pull off again. Praise and cuddling
made us soft, distracted us from the scent of the
mechanical rabbit. My younger brother and I
were raised to be perfectionists, which meant
that if you somehow, against all odds, managed
to finally do something perfectly, you beat yourself up for not having been able to do it years
before. We didn't know that mistakes, imperfec-
tions, and pain were going to turn into strengths
and riches, turn us into Coltrane, Whoopi Gold-
berg, our true selves. Our parents forgot to mention this.

What surprised me when I lit into my uncle was that it made me look so angry to the family. He got to look like his victimized, gentlemanly self, while I came across as Leona Helmsley. Angry was not part of any of my identities—just the opposite, in fact. Angry women got shamed or exiled when I was a child. They got divorced. We were suckered into thinking that jokey, superficial pleasantries was how it was supposed to be in good families, like on TV or next door. People should be functional, grateful, always on, and completely at ease. Had I known how uncomfortable my parents were within themselves, I would have had no hope. I agreed to think both my unmet and my overmet potential were the problems. I agreed to think this to survive. I agreed to be a perfect girl. When I screwed up, that trapdoor opened up at my feet. Decades later I fought my way back to my birthright of ordinary, mixed-up, gorgeous, sometimes lost human. But I hadn't at the time of the dustup with my uncle, so my sense of self took a bit of a hit.

I had the choice of fight, flight, or freeze. I flew, lay low, and got on with the rest of my life.

A few months after I finally stopped drinking, I went to my uncle, hat in hand, all but down on one knee, and asked for forgiveness. I thought he would say: "Wow, that took a lot of courage. Of course I forgive you, my darling." He thanked me and robotically said everything was "fine." I thanked him and we both pretended it was, that this thing was behind us and we could move on. We moved on to where we had started, where he didn't let himself feel much for me or need anything from me. I understood he loved me, in his lifelong anorexic withholding way, and this was some progress: barest minimum, which was a real step up from where we had been.

So diplomat was one of the first identities I relinquished. I mostly gave up trying to get my uncle to be one of those people you miss so much when they die. We both showed up for every family occasion and were unfailingly polite to each other. Now, as he has aged and grown infirm, I offer him rides to other people's funerals and bring plants and books when I visit him in assisted living. I have taken the path of liberation: kindness.

Those old identities keep us so small, and I unconsciously prefer this. It's safe. I make sure everyone knows every time I visit my uncle and what I brought him. But being Dutiful Niece has let me taste something else that I always secretly thought might be there: a rich and inherent decency. (Saying this out loud causes me to tremble.) Also, every so often I notice that I can loosen other identities slightly, too, like tight shoelaces, without having it lead to chaos and death. Contrary to my upbringing, the bigger, more real, and friendlier the world inside me becomes, the safer I feel in the outside world. As above, so below; as inside, so before us. It is not quite yet a world of infinite possibility, but little by little there are more ice cream flavors I may just try.

I continue to visit my uncle. I have active empathy for him now. He sort of laughs at my jokes, or at any rate, he laughed at one of them last week. We even sang a carol together last Christmas in his lobby, one that I hate, "Deck the Halls." To me, it was like Lourdes.

Augustine said that those who sing pray twice.

Empathy says: You and I are made of the same lovely, heartbroken, and screwed-up stuff. You are not an object to me right now. (Maybe I'm not, either! Let me get back to you on this.) Empathy, a moment's compassion, seeing that everyone has equal value, even people who have behaved badly, is as magnetic a force as gratitude. It draws people to us, thus giving us the capacity to practice receiving love, the scariest thing of all, and to experience the curiosity of a child. And, as it turns out, the family is the most incredible, efficient laboratory, in which we can learn to work out the major blocks to these, which of course we got from the family in the first place. If we do the forgiveness work, forgiving our families and ourselves, they become slightly less "them," and we become slightly more "we." It's ultimately about reunion. You might as well start this process at the dinner table. That way you can do this work, for which you were born, in comfortable pants.

Maybe on this side of the grave, you'll never forgive or be able to stand your wife's brother or your sister's child, and that's okay, but don't bank on never. I don't so much anymore. Yes, it's hard hard hard, but when I'm having a good time with my big messy family, I notice and savor it, and I say thank you, that this came from a place of joy and absurdity, that it turns out we have it in us to laugh. And who knows, we may again—later to-day, tomorrow, or in patient, patient time.

Hope

Some days there seems to be little reason for hope, in our families, cities, and world. Well, except for almost everything. The seasons change, a bone mends, Santa Rosa rebuilds after the fire. In the days after a cataclysmic school shooting, thousands of students took to the streets and the public squares. They got us back up onto our feet and changed the world.

Still, we hold our breath. In times of rational and primitive fear, hope has to do push-ups out in the parking lot to stay pumped—and it does. More and more, one hears Dr. King quoted everywhere, of finite disappointment versus in-finite hope. Science, art, community, and nature make manifest that bad will or mistakes can lead to progress, like Bob Ross on his show *The Joy of Painting* reminding us that when we make big mistakes on canvas, we can turn them into birds—"Yeah, they're birds now!"

This is true of almost everything, if one looks up and around, especially in nature and the medicine chest.

For now, just glance out the window at a bird. Those little show-offs with their pure piping song can be the morning's reset button. In a pinch, even absurd, big, silent, gangly birds can do the trick. Two days after the shootings in Parkland, Florida, I bumped into an old friend on the blacktop, where we were sharing feelings of dread and frustration; she was in tears. Sud-denly, we noticed that three tall birds had crept up near us, not ten feet away. They were cranes the size of small people. They had long sharp bills, and my friend waggled her fingers at them, to encourage them to go back to the marsh across the street and not peck us to death. They looked like confused tourists with tiny perplexed eyes: "Why us? We've come a long way. Here we are, minding our own business. . . ." They glared at us and dug in.

It was all so absurd that we burst out laughing, which startled them enough that they walked away huffily. We hugged and parted, somewhat happier. Nothing was solved, and yet hope was restored for two cranky older women who now had a shared story of near-death, by bird.

In my current less-young age, I've learned that almost more than anything, stories hold us together. Stories teach us what is important about life, why we are here and how it is best to behave, and that inside us we have access to treasure, in memories and observations, in imagination. This is what I want to teach the little kids in my writing class, along with the most important thing anyone ever told me: Almost thirty years ago, when I called my mentor Horrible Bonnie at my most toxic and hysterical, having screwed up as a mother, she said to me, "Dearest? Here is the secret: You are preapproved." I kept asking her, "Really?"

This is what I want to teach my niece and my grandson, too, my Sunday school kids, my dearest children, that they are preapproved. This is a come-as-you-are party. Who they were in utero, in kindergarten, in high school, in bed last night, was the very best they could be at the time; was in fact the *only* way they could be at the time. It is okay for them to make bad mistakes and decisions, to write ghastly first drafts. Hey, they're all birds now.

Hope changes as you get a little older, from the hope that this or that happens, to hope in life, old friends, laughter, art, goodness, helpers. I hope and am amazed, some early mornings, at just finding myself alive. I thought as I approached eighteen years old that I was a goner for sure. And here I am, still alive, still here, and often in a good mood. Other early mornings? Not so much. My back aches, my vision fades, I can't concentrate. It's like in the Samuel Beckett novel—"you must go on, I can't go on, I'll go on."

Recently the car needed a new bumper, because I keep backing into the same goddamn tree that insists on standing too close to the driveway and rushing at my car as I pull out, so I dropped it off at the mechanic's and walked down the street to a coffeehouse where a friend would pick me up. As I did, I passed a weedy empty lot where kids were playing a game involving tin cans and a deflated soccer ball. Watching them, I remembered the incredible boredom of childhood, and thought of the effervescent response that I had to playing almost sixty years ago, and that I had today. One of the kids flung the deflated ball through the tin-can goalpost, and I shouted, "Goal, goal," and got some slightly worried glances out of them. Then they went on with their play.

Hope springs from that which is right in front of us, which surprises us, and seems to work.

Of course, we are reduced at times, late at night, no matter how deep our faith in God or Goodness or one another, to quavering aspic. No matter how beautiful our views are of trees and birds and children, there are such scary pronouncements from Washington or our doctors that we can't help hearing the descending tones, of age, global warming, the ticking of the nuclear clock, the heartbeats of the 7.6 billion other people around us. This stuff is scary and it's very real. Yet hope is real, too.

I see my uncle often (the one I accidentally called a scumbutt). Whatever: hey, it's a bird now. Two weeks ago, after he had spent a month in bed and at the hospital with various infections and was near death, he looked up at me as if I were Doris Day when I entered his room. In his whispery, dry-leaf voice, he asked me to come to exercise class with him. We're almost dating at this point. And I am filled with hope and relief because my cousins have asked hospice to enter in. (Hospice is the cavalry. Hospice means that death isn't going to be nearly as bad as you think.) All those years I wished he was the sort of uncle I would miss when he died, and now he is. I will cry and will miss him when he goes, and I am glad. You can't logically get from where we were to where we are now. I think that is what they mean by grace.

The marvelous folksinger Peggy Seeger said once about a cherished friend, "He died, but he is still in my present tense." My younger cousin, who is one of those unusually sweet, faithful people, has advanced colon cancer. Why did this happen? Why her? Well, because as my friend Karen says, this happens to people, and she is a human. I desperately hope her doctors find a way to heal her. My pastor says God always makes a way out of no way, yet the reality is that my cousin may die of this. Mugabe and Assad both seem to be in good health. Why is my cousin sick?

"Why?" is rarely a useful question in the hope business.

By way of illustration: Learned rabbis have disagreed for the last few thousand years on why God was upset enough to bring about the great flood, but it certainly had to do with some humans behaving atrociously to one another, and then having a bunch of vile children. At the time, there were a lot of other myths about great floods in the cultures around Israel—in Babylon, for example. But what is unique to the Bible's version is God's making a covenant afterward, via the rainbow. This is just one of a series of covenants after the breakdown of communications between God and humanity in the form of Adam and Eve, and this one includes animals and all of nature— it's kind of an environmental charter. What if we focus on what the bad event brings forth, like new lands and life and starting over, rather than on the fact that people do horrible things like shoot kids? If we instead focus on the shootings, it's too easy to lose all hope in life and humanity. Yeah, someone *should* hit the great reset button in the sky. Notice that it is God who repents, is converted, at the end of the Noah story. God realizes that He or She overreacted, and promises never to do it again. God gave the people a rainbow as the promise, whenever the light of the sun shines through the rain. If God gets to start over, then it's a free-for-all, even for cowardly lions like me. (But a rainbow—I ask you—how corny is that? And yet every rainbow gets my attention, gets to me, moves me—every time.) Still, why the devastating flood had to happen eludes me.

Why did a fire burn hundreds of thousands

of acres in Santa Rosa and the Wine Country, but not my county, which shares a border, and was just as dry?

Forty miles away, we were under red alert for two weeks that our hills might catch fire. But they never did, despite gale-force winds and not a drop of rain. I walk nearly every day along a path in the hills above my house, above a grove of redwoods. Not one tree was touched by fire.

I breathe in the grove ecstatically every time I see it, and again get to taste one of my favorite flavors of beauty: giant trees, chestnut roan in color, slanting fingers of sun filtering through the branches. There is also the affection and wonder caused by familiarity built over decades of walking beneath these hunky guys. They are so pure, like whales or mountains, as if they were carved. I don't know why we were spared, but I do know that nothing grows as straight as a redwood. Redwoods are one of God's vanities, which you usually see at the microscopic fractal level. I say, well done, Dude.

Trees in any forest have a presence, the beauty of the canopy and glimmers of blue sky like puzzle pieces, but they also have a mystical acoustic effect, due to their physical properties, a hush. You may not share my belief in a Creator, although when humans experience something as powerful as a forest or a rainbow, it is not crazy to assign its existence to a Greater Intelligence. But any hush is a hush, and a hush is usually sacred: there are pockets and patches of great cities where you may find an intense example of this phenomenon. San Francisco's Financial District has it. When I've marched alongside dragons and drums and lions in the Chinese New Year Parade, it was through acoustic tunnels created by the narrow streets and tall buildings, a funnel of quiet.

Tall buildings can be, in their own stony way, gorgeous enough to blow your mind. Architects the world over fill me with hope for humanity and human genius.

Science also fills me with immense hope and relief, and not just the antibiotics I am stockpiling for Armageddon. Friends and family members have died peacefully and pain-free after what used to be devastating illnesses, and some others ended up not dying of them at all. I have a friend with late-stage liver cancer, who is just not going anywhere and is always in a good mood, because she gets to be *alive*. When people talk about what terrible times these are, I remind them of Cipro, antiretrovirals, electric cars, vaccines. Scientists broke the genetic code, decontaminated miles and miles of the Hudson River, cured my older brother of advanced hepatitis C. The human mind, for all its bad press and worse ideas, is as awe-inspiring as Yosemite, as stars.

Our minds are hardwired in many ways to do many things, only half of which from my observations are self-destructive. We can walk without thinking about how we do it, and stay upright. (Well, most of us can, most of the time.) We can recognize a face from the past in a fraction of a second. Our minds can instantly determine whether that face is "friend," "foe," or "unknown" in that same fraction. But if it is someone we've been introduced to that day, we might not be able to remember the person's name ten minutes later. Most of our brains are very good at some things but not so good at others, prewired for certain tasks but not for everything, good enough for most of us and definitely for government work. And then there are the artists, musicians, scientists, painters of light, and physicists—Caravaggio, Rumi, Einstein. As soon as regular people like me can grasp that light is particles, like specks of sand, or that light is waves, like the ripples in water, then scientists step in and prove not only that light is both, but that when we observe light, we change it. I mean, come on, now.

Life is way wilder than I am comfortable with, way farther out, as we used to say, more magnificent, more deserving of awe and, I would add, more benevolent—well-meaning, kindly. Waves and particles, redwoods, poetry, this world of wonders and suffering, great crowds of helpers and humanitarians, here we are alive right now, together. I worry myself sick about the melting ice caps, the escalating arms race, and the polluted air as I look forward with hope to the cleansing rains, the coming spring, the warmth of summer, the student marches. John Lennon said, "Everything will be okay in the end. If it's not okay, it's not the end," and as this has always been true before, we can hope it will be again.

We have all we need to come through. Against all odds, no matter what we've lost, no matter what messes we've made over time, no matter how dark the night, we offer and are offered kindness, soul, light, and food, which create breath and spaciousness, which create hope, sufficient unto the day.

Acknowledgments

I want to thank my editor, Jake Morrissey, for his wise, dogged, loving companionship for the past ten years.

Riverhead Books has been the perfect home for me, so thank you, Geoff Kloske, Katie Freeman, Lydia Hirt, Kevin Murphy, and one of the world's best copy editors, who makes my life a living hell, and saves me from mortification, Anna Jardine.

I love my agent, Sarah Chalfant, at the Wylie Agency so much. We have been through it, huh, girl?

Thank you, everyone at the Steven Barclay Agency, especially His Royal Majesty Steven.

Thank you to my dearest friends who help me so much with my work, every step of the way:

Acknowledgments

Doug Foster, Neshama Franklin, Janine Reid, Neal Allen, Judith Rubin, Mark Yaconelli. Thank you to my Jesuit brothers Tom Weston and Jim Harbaugh, and to Karen Carlson, from whom I've stolen some of my favorite lines.

Thank you to my beloved family, Sam and Jax, my brothers John and Stevo, Clara and Nettie, Tyler and my cousins—the Morgens and Kellogg-Smiths, especially Robby Morgen. Thank you to my sober community, and to the people of St. Andrew Presbyterian Church, Marin City, California. Services at eleven.